Cal Hawthorne

The Teenage Years of Jesus Christ

The Ultimate Pattern for Teenagers Today

By Jerry L. Ross

SWORD OF THE LORD
PUBLISHERS

PO Box 1099
Murfreesboro, TN
37133-1099

All Scripture quotations are from
the King James Bible.

Printed and Bound in the United States of America

To my family: my parents, Robert and Donna Ross, who always point me to Christ; my children, Amanda, Hannah and Tabitha, who bring me great joy; and my wife, Sheryl, who alone shares my soul.

Contents

Introduction vii

1. The Teenage Christ 1

2. The Teenage Christ Increased
   in Wisdom 5

3. The Teenage Christ Increased
   in Maturity 23

4. The Teenage Christ Increased in Favor
   With God 53

5. The Teenage Christ Increased in Favor
   With Man 63

6. The Teenage Christ Remained Subject to
   His Parents 71

7. The Teenage Christ Learned a Wage-
   Earning Skill 77

8. Putting It All Together 89

9. Glorious Even in Failure 94

10. A Brief Word to Parents 101

11. A Brief Word to Youth Workers 111

12. "About My Father's Business" 119

INTRODUCTION

As a Christian teenager, how many times have you thought, *Wouldn't it be great if the Gospels contained some record of the teenage years of Jesus? Why didn't God lead those who penned the Scriptures to include some stories of the Lord as a teenager? What was He like? How did He spend His time? What was important to Him?*

As a youth pastor and parent, I've asked these questions—and more! Perhaps the most repeated statement that I make to the young people of our church is, "The ultimate goal of the Christian life is to be like Jesus!" Wouldn't it be easier for our teens to achieve Christ-likeness if they had some idea what He was like as a teenager?

I have good news. It's right there in the Gospels in black and white. And, as you would expect from Christ, it is life-changing.

In the following pages I will present a scriptural examination of the teenage years of Jesus. I have written this book as if I were writing to one of my own teenagers. I will be straightforward and honest with you and, at times, maybe painfully blunt. I have found that most teens would rather hear the truth from a preacher than have their ears tickled.

Are you ready?

"The ultimate goal of the Christian life is to be like Jesus!"

How about it, teenager? Are you ready for the ultimate challenge?

I
The Teenage Christ

Let's try something. Pick out in your mind someone who has recently graduated from high school, preferably a Christian. Got one? Now, on a piece of paper, list the six things that were the most important to him during his teen years. The items on your list must be determined by the amount of time he spent investing in these activities. Okay? When you're finished, read on.

Like those of the person you've selected, your teen years will also one day be summarized with a similar list. People who know you well will be able to compile a short summary of what was most important to you, based on what you spent the bulk of your time pursuing. They may not include any specific stories, but from the list, we can picture what kind of teenager you were.

For instance, imagine the type of teens that come to mind based on the following short lists:

Teen 1: Football, baseball, basketball, weight lifting, cross-country, track.

Teen 2: Boys, hairstyles, boys, shopping, boys and boys.

Teen 3: Mathematics, chess, science club, computers, astronomy, model planes.

Teen 4: Soul winning, school, church bus route, piano, after-school job, sewing.

Teen 5: Sports, fast food, car, girlfriend, money, TV.

Do you get the picture? No specific stories have been told. Yet from these simple lists we get a sense of what these teenagers were like and how they spent their time—what was most important to them.

In Luke, chapter 2, God gives us a similar list describing the teenage years of Jesus Christ. We know that the items on this list describe specifically His teenage years because they follow the story of Christ in the temple as a twelve-year-old boy. Notice the content of the following passage of Scripture:

> "And he went down with them, and came to Nazareth, and was subject unto them....
>
> "And Jesus increased in wisdom and stature, and in favour with God and man."—Luke 2:51, 52.

These verses give a summary of the activities of Christ in the years following His twelfth year—His teenage years. Consider the following summary list of the main activity and focus of Christ during His teenage years:

The teenage Christ: wisdom, maturity, favor of God, favor of men, subject, work.

The following list expands each of these and adds scriptural support:

1. Increased in wisdom—Luke 2:52.
2. Increased in stature (maturity)—Luke 2:52.
3. Increased in favor with God—Luke 2:52.
4. Increased in favor with men—Luke 2:52.
5. Remained subject to Joseph and His mother—Luke 2:51.
6. Learned a wage-earning skill—Matt. 13:55; Mark 6:3.

I'm not against many of the other interests listed above for our imaginary teenagers. The purpose of this book is not to convince you to eliminate holy interests or healthy hobbies. My intent is to challenge you to make the *priorities* of your teenage years the same as those of the teenage Christ.

2
The Teenage Christ Increased in Wisdom

Don't miss what I am going to say next. **The pursuit of wisdom needs to be the principal priority of your teenage years.** Notice carefully these verses:

> "Get wisdom, get understanding: forget it not; neither decline from the words of my mouth.
>
> "Forsake her not, and she shall preserve thee: love her, and she shall keep thee.
>
> "Wisdom is the principal thing; therefore get wisdom: and with all thy getting get understanding."—Prov. 4:5–7.

Wisdom is the principal thing! Solomon, through the inspiration of God, wrote to his son that of all the things clamoring for his time and attention, he must not neglect to get wisdom; that he must get it *with all his getting.*

I've worked with teenagers for more than twenty years. I've met intelligent teens. I've met many more who were clever, talented and even gifted. I haven't met many who are wise. It is not because they are incapable of becoming wise. Most just do not see the pursuit of wisdom as being important.

One of the greatest misconceptions among teenagers is that wisdom is the result of age and experience alone. There is no doubt that a person who has lived

5

longer has had more opportunity to accumulate wisdom, but wisdom is available to people of all ages.

In Proverbs, chapter 8, Wisdom is crying out, trying to get the attention of men. Notice verse 4: "Unto you, O men, I call; and my voice is to the sons of man."

Wisdom is seeking young people. The entire Book of Proverbs is written to a young man, Solomon's son. At age twelve, it is said of Christ that He was "filled with wisdom" (Luke 2:40).

We have pointed out that from age twelve on, Christ "increased in wisdom." Young people can be wise!

Teenagers can be wise! It does not, however, happen by accident. Anyone who becomes wise must follow the Bible formula for obtaining wisdom.

Let's start by nailing down a clear Bible definition for *wisdom*.

What Is Wisdom?

All true wisdom comes from God. He is Wisdom; therefore, He is the only source of wisdom. The world has always tried to produce a counterfeit and pawn it off as wisdom. The wisdom of this world excludes God and ignores His Word.

> "Where is the wise? where is the scribe? where is the disputer of this world? hath not God made foolish the wisdom of this world?
>
> "For after that in the wisdom of God, the world by wisdom knew not God, it pleased God by the foolishness of preaching to save them that believe."—I Cor. 1:20, 21.

The world by her wisdom chooses to exclude God. Anything that labels itself as wisdom and ignores the clear teachings of the Word of God is not wisdom. It is a counterfeit.

"Now we have received, not the spirit of the world, but the spirit which is of God; that we might know the things that are freely given to us of God.

"Which things also we speak, not in the words which man's wisdom teacheth, but which the Holy Ghost teacheth; comparing spiritual things with spiritual."—I Cor. 2:12, 13.

The Word of God is that which was "freely given to us of God." The Holy Spirit is also given to everyone who trusts Christ as his personal Saviour. As we study the Bible, "comparing spiritual things with spiritual," the Holy Spirit tutors us in God's wisdom. This is God's plan for making His wisdom available to men. Men react in three different ways to this plan. How they react puts them into one of three biblical categories.

Let me introduce to you the three main men of Proverbs: the simple man, the foolish man and the wise man. These three will define *wisdom* for us.

The simple—any person who is ignorant of the teachings of God's Word. Many young people are not reared in church. They are not taught the Bible at home. They have never been consistently exposed to the principles of the Word of God. They are ignorant of what God has given us through His Word.

"For at the window of my house I looked through my casement,

"And beheld among the simple ones, I discerned among the youths, a young man void of understanding."—Prov. 7:6, 7.

The foolish—any person who is taught the principles of God's Word and chooses to reject them. These are young people who sit under the teaching of the Bible in Sunday school and church services. They may even attend a Christian school. They are not ignorant of the teachings of God's Word, but they choose to ignore and reject them.

"The fear of the LORD is the beginning of knowledge: but fools despise wisdom and instruction."—Prov. 1:7.

"A fool hath no delight in understanding."—18:2.

The wise—any person who is taught the principles of God's Word and chooses to believe them and apply them. This young person listens to what is being taught in church. He believes that wisdom is valuable and takes to heart what the Bible teaches. He is willing to adjust his behavior to fit the precepts of God's Word.

"When the wise is instructed, he receiveth knowledge."—Prov. 21:11.

"Hear instruction, and be wise, and refuse it not."—8:33.

On any given Sunday, a Sunday school teacher could have all three types of young people in his class. A young man could be visiting the church for the first time. Up to this point, he has had little, if any, Bible instruction. He is simple.

Next to him may be a teenager who has attended church for years. He is there because his parents make him come. He will daydream during most of the lesson, and the part that he does hear, he has already made up his mind to ignore. He is foolish.

Sitting next to him may be that young man who also has attended church for awhile. He is looking forward to the teaching of God's Word. He wants to learn what the Bible says. Godly instruction, to him, is valuable. He is wise.

Which brings us to our definitions of *wisdom* and the *wise* man:

Wisdom is the ability and willingness to...
...base all of our thoughts, actions and decisions...
...on the principles of the Word of God.

The simple man does not have the ability to do this since he is ignorant of Bible principles.

The foolish man has the ability but not the willingness. His head contains the knowledge, but he has a rebellious heart.

The wise man has both the ability and willingness to live according to the precepts of God's Word. He has invested the time to learn what God wants from him and has a heart that longs to obey and please the Lord.

Jesus Christ as a young Man valued the Word of God and sought out its precious truths. We are told in Luke 4:16 that it was His "custom" to attend the synagogue on the Sabbath. Why? Because that is where the Word of God was read and taught.

We learn from Luke 2:46 that when His family made their annual pilgrimage to Jerusalem, Jesus spent much time in the synagogue listening to and questioning the Bible scholars of His day. Why? Because He hungered for wisdom.

Shortly after Jesus entered the ministry, He returned to Galilee and taught in the temple. The people were amazed at His knowledge and method of teaching. "And the Jews marvelled, saying, How knoweth this man letters, having never learned?" (John 7:15).

Without any formal education, Jesus became an authority on the Scriptures. How? **Because as a teenage boy He made the getting of wisdom the priority of His life.** Maybe other teenagers thought it a bit odd that He spent the time He did studying the Scriptures, asking questions and meditating alone. I don't know. I do know that He spent His teen years doing those things that enable one to 'increase in wisdom.'

How about you? Is wisdom important to you? It was to the teenage Christ. Are you willing to take time to do those things that will cause you to 'increase in wisdom' during your teen years?

The Bible Formula for Increasing in Wisdom

"Wisdom is the principal thing; therefore get wisdom: and with all thy getting get understanding."—Prov. 4:7.

God puts upon us the responsibility of getting wisdom. He requires effort from us if we are to be rewarded with His wisdom. The Bible is very clear on what we must do to obtain wisdom. God is going to make us work for it. Salvation is free, but wisdom comes with a price tag. It is not handed out like candy to the immature and undedicated. Welcome to real life, my friend.

The teenager who is given a car by his parents seldom values it as he should. But let that same teenager work and save money and earn that car himself, then he will value it.

"Happy is the man that findeth wisdom, and the man that getteth understanding.

"For the merchandise of it is better than the merchandise of silver, and the gain thereof than fine gold.

"She is more precious than rubies: and all the things thou canst desire are not to be compared unto her."—Prov. 3:13–15.

Wisdom is a valuable commodity. God expects you to want it badly enough to put out the effort to obtain it. Here is what He requires if you wish to increase in wisdom:

1. Fear the Lord. All wisdom comes from God. If we are to increase in wisdom, our relationship to Him must be right. So the starting point for receiving either knowledge or wisdom is establishing a right relationship with Him.

> *"The fear of the LORD is the beginning of knowledge."*—Prov. 1:7.

> *"The fear of the LORD is the beginning of wisdom."*—9:10.

> *"The fear of the LORD is the instruction of wisdom."*—15:33.

You must start at the beginning. The young person who wants wisdom needs to understand that God deserves our respect and awe. He has illustrated throughout His Word two undeniable facts: He loves people, and He hates sin. God is to be both loved and feared. This is not a contradiction. The teenager who views God as one who overlooks sin or winks at sin does not understand who God is. Without a fear of God, you will never become wise. This is the starting place.

2. Be teachable. Nothing prevents the flow of wisdom faster than a man's pride. In order to receive God's wisdom, we must trade in *our* "wisdom."

> *"Be not wise in thine own eyes: fear the LORD, and depart from evil."*—Prov. 3:7.

> *"Cease from thine own wisdom."*—23:4.

We must approach the Bible humbly as a student who is willing to believe whatever the Bible teaches. Too many times our preconceived notions about what we already believe to be true prevent us from being willing to accept clear biblical instruction. We approach the Bible determined to make it back up what we have already accepted as truth, instead of adjusting our beliefs to its teachings. So be teachable.

3. Pray for wisdom. The Bible clearly instructs us to ask God for wisdom.

> *"If any of you lack wisdom, let him ask of God, that giveth to all men liberally, and upbraideth not; and it shall be given him."*—Jas. 1:5.

Wisdom should be near the top of your prayer list. Prayer is an act of humility. Admit to God that you lack wisdom and ask Him for His wisdom.

4. Study the Scriptures. When you become a teenager, it is time to graduate from reading the Bible to studying the Bible. This is what has been "freely given to us." This is the written wisdom of God.

> *"Study to shew thyself approved unto God, a workman that needeth not to be ashamed, rightly dividing the word of truth."*—II Tim. 2:15.

It was said of Christ that at age twelve He was filled with wisdom (Luke 2:40); after age twelve He increased in wisdom (vs. 52). The first was the result of the actions of others; the second, the result of His own actions.

For the first twelve years, most children are "filled with wisdom" by their parents, their teachers and their pastors. They are spoon-fed. When a young person enters his teenage years, he needs to decide to build on that foundation and 'increase in wisdom.'

It's time to start feeding yourself! We need a generation of young people who will get serious about studying God's Word. Invest in a good Bible concordance, get a notebook and a pencil and begin "comparing spiritual things with spiritual." Wisdom is God's reward for your willingness to search and study the Scriptures.

> "If thou seekest her as silver, and searchest for her as for hid treasures:
>
> "Then shalt thou understand the fear of the LORD, and find the knowledge of God.
>
> "For the LORD giveth wisdom: out of his mouth cometh knowledge and understanding."—Prov. 2:4-6.

There are many ways to study the Bible. In chapter 3, I will show you an effective way to study the Scriptures. Your pastor or parents may help you with other ways.

5. Receive instruction. God, in His wisdom, has provided you with parents, grandparents, teachers and a pastor. All of these people are commanded by God to teach you wisdom. So having the right attitude toward instruction is essential if you are to increase in wisdom.

> "Give instruction to a wise man, and he will be yet wiser: teach a just man, and he will increase in learning."—Prov. 9:9.
>
> "When the wise is instructed, he receiveth knowledge."—21:11.

"I don't like people telling me what to do!" seems to be the theme of a rebellious generation. Having the right attitude toward instruction will put you leaps and bounds ahead of your peers. While they, in their stubbornness, insist on learning everything the "hard way," you can learn from those who have gone before and avoid many mistakes and heartaches.

6. Seek counsel. A wise teenager takes a step beyond personal study and public instruction. He also seeks private counsel.

> "Hear counsel, and receive instruction, that thou mayest be wise in thy latter end."—Prov. 19:20.

"For by wise counsel thou shalt make thy war: and in multitude of counsellors there is safety."—24:6.

Carefully select wise individuals from whom you can seek counsel. Do not seek advice from someone who seems to have a great deal of Bible knowledge yet does not live a godly life. The foolish man knows much about the Bible, but he fails to apply what he knows to everyday life. God is not impressed with how much Bible you *know* but with how much Bible you *live*. Select godly adults who will give you biblical advice, and pick their brains—not their hearts. If you have Christian parents, take advantage of their wisdom.

7. Accept rebuke. Man's pride resists rebuke. However, receiving rebuke is a necessary ingredient in gaining wisdom.

"Reprove not a scorner, lest he hate thee: rebuke a wise man, and he will love thee."—Prov. 9:8.

"As an earring of gold, and an ornament of fine gold, so is a wise reprover upon an obedient ear."—25:12.

"The ear that heareth the reproof of life abideth among the wise."—5:31.

Nothing tells me more about the maturity and wisdom of a teenager than how he or she handles rebuke.

I am the principal of our Christian school. From time to time it is my responsibility to rebuke a student.

Years ago a young man transferred to our school as a senior. He had attended public school most of his life and was unfamiliar with a lot of the rules and common courtesies required in a Christian school.

He was in my office a lot those first few weeks. I'll never forget the first time he was there. Some of his conduct had been unacceptable; I was pretty tough on him, and I explained why. I didn't have six or seven years to bring him along slowly, so when I needed to correct something, we would face it head on.

His reaction? He listened intently to all I had to say, then when I was finished, he asked to say something.

"Pastor Jerry, I came to this school my senior year because I want to serve God with my life. If you see anything—anything—that I am doing wrong, please let me know."

What an amazing attitude! I had the pleasure of watching that young man graduate and go on to a blessed life of service to God.

I compare him with many teenagers who have been so spoiled, so coddled, that they cannot handle the slightest rebuke. They pout when their parents correct them and complain when anyone in authority tries to help them become wise through rebuke. I have worked with young people long enough to see the end of that road—a life of failure and excuses. The young person who bristles at reproof is playing the fool.

Rebuke is a part of life, a necessary part of teaching and preaching (II Tim. 4:2; Titus 2:15). It is one of the duties of the Holy Spirit. Wise is the teenager who is thankful to those who love him enough to rebuke him.

8. Go soul winning. The theme of the Bible is the redemption of men. The Great Commission is a mandate for every Christian to share the Gospel with the lost. So to gain the wisdom of God, become a soul winner.

"The fruit of the righteous is a tree of life; and he that winneth souls is wise."—Prov. 11:30.

Many of the teachings of the Bible will not make sense unless you are actively involved in personal evangelism. God opens His Word to those who will become laborers in the harvest fields and withholds many things from those who refuse.

9. Choose wise companions. Someone once said, "Show me a man's friends today, and I will show you what he will be tomorrow." God says it a little more strongly:

> "He that walketh with wise men shall be wise: but a companion of fools shall be destroyed."—Prov. 13:20.

I have watched many good young people be destroyed because of bad company. So to increase in wisdom, select wise companions. Review the definitions of *wisdom* and of the *wise man*. It is better to be alone than to develop friendships with fools.

> "Go from the presence of a foolish man, when thou perceivest not in him the lips of knowledge.
>
> "The wisdom of the prudent is to understand his way: but the folly of fools is deceit."—Prov. 14:7, 8.

Be able to identify a foolish person and avoid him. You may be tempted to say, "But isn't that judging someone?"

God has commanded us to flee from the presence of such a one. He has also provided us with a detailed description of the characteristics of the foolish man: "The wisdom of the prudent is to understand his way."

God expects us to choose friends based on outward evidences of their wisdom—and to avoid them if they display the characteristics of a fool.

Below is a list of the characteristics of the foolish man as found in the book of Proverbs.

Identifying the Foolish by How He Acts

A foolish person ignores reproof. He refuses to be corrected and hates the one who tries to help him.

> *"A reproof entereth more into a wise man than an hundred stripes into a fool."*—Prov. 17:10.

> *"Reprove one that hath understanding, and he will understand knowledge."*—19:25.

A foolish person despises instruction. He is not humble enough to admit that he needs instruction. He thinks he already knows everything.

> *"A fool despiseth his father's instruction."*—Prov. 15:5.

> *"The fear of the LORD is the beginning of knowledge: but fools despise wisdom and instruction."*—1:7.

A foolish person perceives himself as always right. He thinks he knows more than his parents, his teachers, his pastor—even God.

> *"The way of a fool is right in his own eyes: but he that hearkeneth unto counsel is wise."*—Prov. 12:15.

> *"A wise man feareth, and departeth from evil: but the fool rageth, and is confident."*—14:16.

A foolish person sees mischief as sport. He thinks it's funny to cause trouble. When corrected, he reacts by saying, "I was just kidding. Can't you take a joke?" Causing trouble is not a joke.

> *"It is as sport to a fool to do mischief: but a man of understanding hath wisdom."*—Prov. 10:23.

A foolish person makes a mockery of sin. He thinks it amusing when someone says or does something unholy or perverse.

"Fools make a mock at sin: but among the righteous there is favour."—Prov. 14:9.

A foolish person is quick-tempered. If you cannot control your temper, you will all your life be labeled a fool by those who know God's Word.

"A fool's wrath is presently known: but a prudent man covereth shame."—Prov. 12:16.

"He that is soon angry dealeth foolishly."—14:17.

"A stone is heavy, and the sand weighty; but a fool's wrath is heavier than them both."—27:3.

A foolish person meddles in the affairs of others. He is a gossiper and a busybody.

"It is an honour for a man to cease from strife: but every fool will be meddling."—Prov. 20:3.

A foolish person despises his parents. He breaks the heart of his mother and shames his father's name.

"A wise son maketh a glad father: but a foolish man despiseth his mother."—Prov. 15:20.

"A foolish son is the calamity of his father."—19:13.

Identifying the Foolish by What He Says

A foolish person slanders others. The only way he can feel good about himself is to tear down everyone around him.

"...he that uttereth a slander, is a fool."—Prov. 10:18.

A foolish person is double-tongued. He will speak well to you with lying lips while secretly despising you.

"He that hideth hatred with lying lips...is a fool."—Prov. 10:18.

A foolish person has perverse lips. Here, "perverse" means distorted or crooked. He does not have the integrity to tell a story without distorting the facts with the bias of his own agenda.

"Better is the poor that walketh in his integrity, than he that is perverse in his lips, and is a fool."—Prov. 19:1.

A foolish person quickly speaks his mind. His philosophy is, "If I think it, I should say it." He does not think something through before speaking.

"A fool uttereth all his mind: but a wise man keepeth it in till afterwards."—Prov. 29:11.

"Seest thou a man that is hasty in his words? there is more hope of a fool than of him."—29:20.

A foolish person's tongue holds forth a rod of pride. He has "I" problems. He will always turn the conversation back to himself, which, by the way, is his favorite topic.

"In the mouth of the foolish is a rod of pride: but the lips of the wise shall preserve them."—Prov. 14:3.

A foolish person talks a lot of foolishness. Earlier we defined a foolish man as someone who has been taught the Bible but refuses to submit himself to its precepts. Listen to those around you who regularly attend your church, your youth group or your Christian school. Mark those who make it a habit to criticize the Bible standards of separation from the world, who scoff at the preaching and who make fun of those who are trying to live by the Word of God.

"A prudent man concealeth knowledge: but the heart of fools proclaimeth foolishness."—Prov. 12:23.

"The tongue of the wise useth knowledge aright: but the mouth of fools poureth out foolishness."—15:2.

"The heart of him that hath understanding seeketh knowledge: but the mouth of fools feedeth on foolishness."—15:14.

A foolish person is contentious. He is always looking for an argument, always looking for a fight. This person doesn't seem to be able to be happy unless he has caused some kind of contention. He does a lot of damage in a church.

"A fool's lips enter into contention, and his mouth calleth for strokes."—Prov. 18:6.

My teenage friend, you *must* become wise enough to choose the right companions! The warning of God is very clear: wise companions will help make you wise, but foolish companions will destroy you.

As you review the above list, it is always good to start with yourself. Are there foolish attributes that have become habits in your own life? Then confess these to God. Ask Him to help you behave wisely in all things.

Then examine those with whom you spend most of your time. Be honest with yourself. A teenager once told me, "No one has a right to choose my friends for me." I beg to disagree. God has every right to teach you how to select wise companions. By the way, the young lady who made that statement no longer goes to church. Her "friends" influenced her to stop attending church, to stop going soul winning and to stop serving God. She is now involved in an immoral, ungodly lifestyle. It is now tomorrow, and she is now what they are.

Stop here and review the nine biblical steps to increase in wisdom. Schedule your time and discipline your life so that you will begin now to make each of these a regular part of your week.

Congratulations! You are on your way to achieving the ultimate goal of the Christian life. You are on your way to becoming like the teenage Christ.

3

The Teenage Christ Increased in Maturity

"And Jesus increased in wisdom and stature, and in favour with God and man."—Luke 2:52.

The second characteristic of the teenage years of Christ was an increase in "stature." According to *Strong's Concordance,* the word *stature* means "maturity." During His teenage years, Jesus matured. Physically, mentally and socially He "grew up."

The other day I was listening to a well-known psychiatrist on the radio give advice to a twenty-three-year-old call-in listener. This young man, involved in an illicit affair with a twenty-year-old woman, was bemoaning the fact that she had recently broken off the affair and was now involved with another. The radio psychiatrist made a statement that amazed me: "You made a mistake in getting involved with this woman. At age twenty-three, you're going to make mistakes. The twenties are years when you grow up."

I usually don't talk to the radio, but I said, "No! Not only is it not true, but it could be the most dangerous philosophy being taught today!"

I turned off the radio and began to meditate upon the Scriptures I had studied in preparing to write this chapter. God taught me some great truths that day while driving home.

The world says, "You can grow up in your twenties." The world says, "The teenage years are for fun, frolicking and foolishness. You can become responsible later."

Why is this philosophy of the world so dangerous?

Your character is developed during your teenage years. You cannot just flip a switch at age twenty and say, "Now I am going to start being mature. Now I am going to start to be Christlike." Habits developed during your teens will have now become part of your character; it will, by then, be who you are. Change becomes increasingly difficult by this time in life.

Christ's example teaches us that the teenage years are for preparation. Maturity should become a primary goal of your life, beginning at the age of twelve. The Bible teaches that God divides mankind into three basic age groups: children, young men or women, and the aged men or women.

We have created a new group called teenagers. In Bible times, a child's twelfth birthday was a milestone, a beginning, the doorway to adulthood. At this age, he picked up the mantle of maturity.

Most of life's major decisions are made from eighteen to twenty-four years of age. During these years, most people choose their career, a college, their companions, their mate. To wait until you are in your twenties to begin to mature will mean you will be ill prepared to make these major decisions.

Wrong decisions in these major areas will result in spending much of your life trying to fix these "wrongs" and dealing with the consequences of these poor decisions. The young person who understands that he is to begin to develop in maturity at age twelve will be prepared to make wise, godly decisions as a young adult.

Maturity—Putting Away the Three "Childish Things"

"When I was a child, I spake as a child, I understood as a child, I thought as a child: but when I became a man, I put away childish things."—I Cor. 13:11.

Maturity affects speech, understanding and thinking.

Hey, teenager, it's time to grow up! Christ did not spend His teenage years being immature and childish. You don't have to either.

Developing Excellent Speech

Rare is the teenager who has taken the time to discover and follow Bible principles for proper speaking. What we say says volumes about who we really are. We are reminded in Matthew 12:34, "For out of the abundance of the heart the mouth speaketh."

Other Christians are influenced by what we say. The unsaved are listening. God hears all. Words are powerful! They can be used to bring joy and encouragement to those around us. Unfortunately, they can also be the source of devastation and hurt.

"And the tongue is a fire, a world of iniquity: so is the tongue among our members, that it defileth the whole body, and setteth on fire the course of nature; and it is set on fire of hell."

"But the tongue can no man tame; it is an unruly evil, full of deadly poison."—Jas. 3:6, 8.

"The words of a talebearer are as wounds, and they go down into the innermost parts of the belly."—Prov. 18:8.

How important that we enlist the Lord's help in taming this dangerous member! How important that we pass personal laws concerning when and how we use our tongues! These laws should be based on clear Bible principles.

Notice the wisdom of the virtuous woman described in Proverbs 31:

"She openeth her mouth with wisdom; and in her tongue is the law of kindness."—Vs. 26.

She decided to open her mouth only in wisdom. She passed laws concerning the use of her tongue, laws that she would live by. Every law has a corresponding penalty that is applied when that law is broken or ignored. These penalties she would enforce upon herself because of her character, virtue and self-discipline. What a Christian!

How about it, teenager? How important is it to you to become like Jesus? Christlikeness—is it your ultimate goal? With the help of the Lord, you can develop biblical speech, or "excellent speech."

"Hear; for I will speak of excellent things; and the opening of my lips shall be right things."—Prov. 8:6.

"Excellent speech becometh not a fool."—17:7.

Consider the following laws. Study for yourself their biblical accuracy. When you are convinced of them, pass these laws and live by them. When they are broken, punish yourself. Make the punishment severe enough so you will not want to break them. This is self-discipline. This is maturity.

The Ten Laws of Excellent Speech

I. Speak Sparingly

"He that hath knowledge spareth his words."—Prov. 17:27.

26

"In the multitude of words there wanteth not sin: but he that refraineth his lips is wise."—10:19.

My Grandpa Ogle used to tell me, "Son, you can't learn nothing with your mouth open!" His grammar may have been lacking, but his instruction was right! The wise teenager spends more time listening than talking.

The more you talk, the more likely you will be to sin. In Proverbs 10:19, the word "wanteth" means "lacketh." In a multitude of words there lacketh not sin. Idle talk *always* leads to sin. *Always!*

Unplanned telephone conversations between Christians have produced as much sin as all of the taverns in America put together.

"Dad, can I call So-and-so?"

"Why? What do you need to ask her?"

"Nothing. I just want to talk."

No. Idle, unplanned conversation leads to sin. The longer the conversation, the greater is the sin.

I have had teenagers tell me that they spend hours each evening on the phone with friends. These are, without exception, also the same teenagers who struggle with having a good attitude. A very wise man once told me, "Weak minds talk about people; average minds talk about things; great minds talk about ideas." Unplanned conversations *always* deteriorate into gossip. *Always!*

If you want to develop excellent speech, eliminate any situation where you are prone just to sit and talk.

I am shocked at how many teenagers are allowed to have telephones in their rooms. A wise teenager will unplug that phone, take it to his parents and say,

"Being like Jesus and developing excellent speech are more important to me than having this in my room. Please do not allow me to change my mind on this decision."

2. Speak Only After Thinking

"Seest thou a man that is hasty in his words? there is more hope of a fool than of him."—Prov. 29:20.

"Wherefore, my beloved brethren, let every man be swift to hear, slow to speak, slow to wrath."—Jas. 1:19.

Take time to think before you speak. When you finish reading all ten of these laws, I suggest you stop and memorize them. It would be wise to run them through your mind before you speak.

Most people are afraid of silence. When someone asks a question, they feel obligated to answer quickly. Be careful. The Bible instructs us to be slow to speak. Ask yourself this question, *Is this something that I should be talking about?* If not, don't answer!

Not every question asked should be answered. Jesus often simply ignored "loaded" questions. Often He would answer a question with a question. Not everyone who asks a question does so because he really wants your knowledge. Be slow to speak.

"I don't know" is a very good answer and probably should be used more than it is. Have you ever been asked a question, given an answer, then later thought of a much better answer? I have. It is often wise to ask the person to allow you time to think about your answer before you give it, especially when asked advice on something important to him.

3. Speak Honestly

"Wherefore putting away lying, speak every man

truth with his neighbour."—Eph. 4:25.

"He that speaketh truth sheweth forth righteousness: but a false witness deceit."—Prov. 12:17.

An important "law of your lips" is the truth law. Never allow yourself to speak a lie. Proverbs, chapter 6, contains a list of seven things that God hates, things that are an abomination unto Him. Two of these involve the sin of lying. I am shocked at how many Christian teenagers I have met have already become habitual liars. Speak only the truth.

Speaking honestly involves what you do and don't say. If you were sworn in to testify in a court of law, you would be required to place your hand on the Bible and answer this question: "Do you promise to tell the truth, the whole truth, and nothing but the truth, so help you God?" The reason you are asked this three-fold question on truthfulness is that it is not the truth if it is a partial truth or an embellished truth.

"Dad, So-and-so did such and such to me at school today!" But you leave out the part about the unkind comment you had made earlier to this person. You also add a few actions or words to make what he did seem worse than it was. So you are a liar. You say you didn't lie. Yes, you lied when you did not tell the truth, the whole truth, and nothing but the truth. Excellence demands personal honesty.

4. Speak With Grace

"Let your speech be alway with grace, seasoned with salt."—Col. 4:6.

This fourth law follows the honesty law on purpose. Although we should only speak the truth, not all that is true should be spoken.

Grace is commonly defined as "unmerited favor," favor shown to us when we do not deserve it. If it were not for grace, none of us would be saved. Speaking with grace means that we should show the same type favor to others that we have received from God.

Never speak an unkind truth. Salt preserves. It does not destroy. When speaking of others, season your words with grace.

5. Speak Only Acceptable Words

"Let the words of my mouth, and the meditation of my heart, be acceptable in thy sight, O LORD, my strength, and my redeemer."—Ps. 19:14.

Filter every statement through the sieve of God's acceptance. Test every word against what He would deem correct. This will eliminate crude, vulgar, perverse and even questionable words and phrases.

Be especially careful of slang words. Many of these are derived from sexually explicit terms.

6. Speak Appropriately

"A word fitly spoken is like apples of gold in pictures of silver."—Prov. 25:11.

An appropriate statement is a work of art. Often we say the right thing at the wrong time.

"To every thing there is a season, and a time to every purpose under the heaven."—Eccles. 3:1.

A good question to ask yourself before you speak is, What time is it? Humor is a wonderful tool, but it is not always appropriate. Rebuke is often needed, but timing is everything. It is important not only to check if what you are about to say is right but also if it is the right time to say it.

7. Speak Respectfully

"Rebuke not an elder, but intreat him as a father; and the younger men as brethren;

"The elder women as mothers; the younger as sisters, with all purity."—I Tim. 5:1, 2.

Consider carefully the tone in which you address people. Never sound as if you are rebuking someone older than you. If you disagree with someone in authority, approach him privately and speak to him with the same respect you would show your father. Entreat him.

Two teenagers have a question about a decision I have made. Neither is happy, and both want to convince me to change my mind or at least allow them to present their case.

The first approaches me in front of other students and, with a disrespectful tone, begins, "I don't think you're being fair about..." Whether or not he is right about my decision, he has already lost his case because he is wrong in his attitude.

The second teenager asks to talk to me privately at my convenience, then politely and respectfully asks me to clarify for him the decision I have made. I may not change my decision, but I guarantee you, if I can make any allowance for that young person, I will.

What's the difference? One rebuked; one entreated. The difference is respect.

This verse also warns teens to guard against using suggestive statements or a suggestive tone with members of the opposite sex. Address other young people as you would your brother or sister "with all purity." To do otherwise is to show a lack of respect for them and for God.

8. Never Speak Evil of Another

"Speak not evil one of another, brethren."—Jas. 4:11.

"Speak evil of no man."—Titus 3:2.

This goes beyond just saying something that is true but negative. The word "evil" in these verses speaks to motive. These verses are saying, "Don't purposely say anything designed to defame someone. Do not be a reputation assassin."

Carnality and pride are the motives behind any Christian who publicly or privately spreads any story, true or false, that blackens that person's reputation. The Bible is very clear on this. The preachers I have the most respect for, when criticized, never retaliate. Instead, they obey the Bible and overcome evil with good. Never speak evil of another person.

9. Never Praise Yourself

"Let another man praise thee, and not thine own mouth; a stranger, and not thine own lips."—Prov. 27:2.

Nothing turns people off faster than the man who is a "legend in his own mind." Be of a humble spirit and let God do the exalting.

10. Speak the Gospel Boldly

"For I am not ashamed of the gospel of Christ: for it is the power of God unto salvation to every one that believeth."—Rom. 1:16.

When God gives you an opportunity to witness, give it all you've got! Always be ready to share your testimony with someone who is without Christ.

Excellent speech is the hallmark of excellent character. I dare you to yield your tongue to the use of God.

In doing so, you will achieve a level of maturity and discipline that will serve you well throughout your life.

"If any man offend not in word, the same is a perfect man, and able also to bridle the whole body."—Jas. 3:2.

Deepen Your Biblical Understanding

Paul makes it plain that there is a difference between childish and mature understanding.

"When I was a child, I spake as a child, I understood as a child, I thought as a child: but when I became a man, I put away childish things."—I Cor. 13:11.

The "childish things" include childish—immature or undeveloped—understanding. An important priority of your teenage years is to perfect your understanding.

Understanding involves thinking. It is the ability to reason. For the child of God, it is the ability to base our reaction to life's circumstances and situations on intellect rather than emotion. Understanding is when scriptural thoughts replace emotional reaction. This does not eliminate emotion; instead, it channels our emotions into compliance with God's emotions. Understanding is the maturity to see a situation as God sees it, and feel about it as He feels.

In the Book of Proverbs, again and again Solomon encourages his son to increase in three areas: knowledge, understanding and wisdom. Notice how these three attributes are connected:

Knowledge: learning *what* God wants me to do.

Understanding: learning *why* God wants me to do it.

Wisdom: learning *how* to do what God wants me to do.

From the time you were born until you reach the

"magic" age of twelve, most of your biblical instruction is focused on seeing that you receive knowledge and wisdom. These two attributes are strongly related. Reread their above definitions. Knowledge is learning *what* to do. Wisdom is learning *how* to do what God wants you to do.

In Sunday school and in preaching services, you have been taught what is right and that you have an obligation to do what is right. Your parents have been commanded both to teach you—verbal instruction on *what* God expects from you—and train you—practical instruction on *how* to do what God expects from you. This is the focus of the first twelve years of a child's development. They may not have spent a great deal of time up to this point telling you *why* you are to do what God wants you to do. That's okay. Your teenage years are for perfecting your understanding, for increasing in stature.

Up to this point, the answer to the question, "Why?" may have been, "Because I said so." Again, that's okay. A child who has not learned that wisdom is instantly obeying Bible knowledge will never be mature enough to attain understanding. God will never explain *why* to a person who *won't*.

At age twelve, Jesus was already filled with knowledge and wisdom:

> "And the child grew, and waxed strong in spirit, filled with wisdom: and the grace of God was upon him."— Luke 2:40.

In the following verses of this same chapter, Jesus is in the temple conversing with the "doctors," the biblical scholars of His time, "both hearing them, and asking them questions."

He was filled with wisdom. By definition, He was also already filled with knowledge: no one can know *how* to do *what* he does not know to do. He had knowledge. He had wisdom. Now He was after understanding. He wanted to know *why*. It was time to attain to biblical understanding or mature understanding.

Hey, teenager, it's time to start developing your biblical intellect; time to begin to separate mentally, to distinguish, to consider, to understand the meaning of knowledge; time to acquire biblical reasons for doing what you have been taught to do.

We call this forming Bible convictions.

> "But continue thou in the things which thou hast learned and hast been assured of, knowing of whom thou hast learned them;
>
> "And that from a child thou hast known the holy scriptures, which are able to make thee wise unto salvation through faith which is in Christ Jesus."—II Tim. 3:14, 15.
>
> "Let no man despise thy youth....
>
> "Till I come, give attendance to reading, to exhortation, to doctrine....
>
> "Meditate upon these things; give thyself wholly to them; that thy profiting may appear to all.
>
> "Take heed unto thyself, and unto the doctrine; continue in them: for in doing this thou shalt both save thyself, and them that hear thee."—I Tim. 4:12–16.

If you have been reared in a good church, you have been exposed to Bible truths. Like Timothy, from childhood you have known the holy Scriptures. You have been taught the stories of the Bible in Sunday school. You have won prizes and ribbons for Bible memory. Bible drills are your speciality—you can find Zephaniah 2:4 faster than anyone else in your class! The Ten

Commandments, the Lord's Prayer, Psalm 23, the books of the Old and New Testaments in order—you can quote them all. You can finish your Sunday school teacher's lesson for her and know if she left out any part of the story. You have learned many Bible truths. But have you become assured of them? Have you given yourself wholly to them? Have you adopted Bible convictions?

In the above Scriptures, God is encouraging young people to go beyond a head knowledge of the truths of His Word. He is saying, "You have learned; now become convinced of My truths. You have been taught; now embrace My truths. You have read; now give yourself wholly to these truths. Make them yours. You know with your head; now believe with your heart!"

It seems that every preacher has used the illustration that many people miss Heaven by sixteen inches— the distance between your head and your heart. I also believe that most Christians miss the will of God for their lives by the same distance. Very few of you teenagers reading this book could tell me why you believe what you say you believe. The reason is very simple: *You never study the Bible for yourself.*

I have watched teenagers grow up. I've worked with them for twenty years. See if the following scenario sounds familiar to you.

A teenager is reared in a good home and a Bible-preaching church. He is taught what is right to do and is expected to do it. For the most part, he complies— at least outwardly. He is a part of the youth group, maybe even goes to the Christian school. He graduates. Within a few months, he has moved away from home. He no longer attends church. He develops a lifestyle opposite of that in which he has been reared.

What happened? In most cases, he was taught what to do, he was even taught how to do it, but he never matured in his understanding. He insisted on holding onto his *childish* understanding.

It is a lot easier simply to announce that you do not agree with the Bible teachings of your parents and pastor than it is to prove from the Scriptures that they are wrong. Where are the Bible principles upon which you are basing your life? Get out the Book!

"Brethren, be not children in understanding: howbeit in malice be ye children, but in understanding be men."—I Cor. 14:20.

It's time to grow up in your understanding of the Scriptures. Your teenage years should be spent studying the Word of God, not in an attempt to find excuses for living the way you want but in an effort to find out the will of God in every matter as revealed in His Word. Through the careful study of God's Word, you will become assured of the things you have learned. Each Bible truth will become yours. The Holy Spirit will convince you of its accuracy and will help you to embrace each one as your own. But first you must study.

A Guide to Studying the Bible

"Study to shew thyself approved unto God, a workman that needeth not to be ashamed, rightly dividing the word of truth."—II Tim. 2:15.

The Bible clearly commands every Christian to study the Bible—not just to read it. Here are some simple steps to help you begin to study the Bible:

Step 1: Enlist the help of a tutor—the Holy Spirit. If you are saved, He dwells within you and wants to help you understand the Bible. Talk to Him. The Holy Spirit is a Person, not an "it." He is as much a part of the Godhead as the Father or the Son. He has been given to us to teach us. Pray and ask Him to reveal truth to you as you study God's Word.

Step 2: Spend time gathering knowledge. Select a subject and do a word study. You will need a good Bible concordance. For example, let's use the word *meditation*. By using an exhaustive concordance, you will find that there are twenty verses in the Bible that use the word "meditate" or "meditation." Look up these verses and write them out so you can view them together. This takes time and work! Don't take shortcuts.

Gather all that the Bible says on a subject before dividing this information and drawing conclusions. To do less is to risk being inaccurate in your interpretation and beliefs.

Step 3: Rightly divide the information. Organize the information found in these verses into proper categories. A good journalist or detective always asks the same questions: who, what, where, when and how? From the information included in these verses ask:

Who is this verse written to (to the saved or to the lost)?
What am I to meditate about?
Where am I to meditate?
When am I to meditate?
How will I benefit from meditation?

The answers to these questions are found in these verses. Remember, this is not an exercise of human intellect but a teaching exercise between the Spirit of God and the spirit of man.

Step 4: Define Bible words that are unfamiliar. A

good Greek and Hebrew dictionary is provided in the back of your *Strong's Exhaustive Concordance*. Other good Bible dictionaries are on the market.

Step 5: Compare verses. Remember, the Bible *never contradicts* itself; instead, it *completes* itself. The best commentary on the Bible is the Bible.

Step 6: Meditate on these verses. This is where the Holy Spirit has the great opportunity to teach us. If there is something unclear to you, pray and ask Him to guide you.

Step 7: Seek wise counsel. Most men of God enjoy helping a young person discover the truth of the Scriptures. Those who have spent their lives studying the Bible can help you with difficult passages. Also, beware of "never-before-discovered truths." Before you announce that you have found a doctrine never before discovered, talk to your preacher. Often young Bible students miss qualifying truths from related Scriptures.

Step 8: Make personal application of the truths you have learned. The Bible is designed to change us. God is not impressed with how much Bible you know but with how much of it you *live*. Never forget that! Knowledge gathered but not applied will rot and stink like day-old manna. If you are unwilling to apply the wisdom the Holy Spirit teaches you, then He will cease to tutor you further.

Step 9: Keep a notebook. Write down the principles that you have been taught. Review them often and remember that they are more precious than rubies, more important than silver or gold. They will mean more because you did the work.

Step 10: Be thankful. Praise the Lord and thank Him for His Word, His blessed Holy Spirit, and for teaching you His wisdom.

Personal Bible study, combined with the preaching and teaching you receive each week, helps you discover the "why's" of your beliefs and keeps you from being deceived by false doctrine and worldliness.

"That we henceforth be no more children, tossed to and fro, and carried about with every wind of doctrine, by the sleight of men, and cunning craftiness, whereby they lie in wait to deceive;

"But speaking the truth in love, may grow up into him in all things, which is the head, even Christ."—Eph. 4:14,15.

The teenager who studies the Bible for himself develops mental depth and spiritual insight beyond his years. Let's look at some wonderful benefits to developing your understanding during your teenage years.

Benefits of Developing Mature Understanding

1. An Excellent Spirit

"A man of understanding is of an excellent spirit."— Prov. 17:27.

A teenager who begins to do right based on an understanding of God's Word eliminates the cause of rebellion. Dad and Mom are no longer "making" you do what is right. The preacher becomes your friend because he is helping you to grow in your understanding. Your desire to mature in your understanding makes you a delight, a blessing, to all those who teach you.

2. Happiness

"Happy is the man that findeth wisdom, and the man that getteth understanding."—Prov. 3:13.

The Teenage Christ Increased in Maturity

Maturity brings happiness. Show me an immature teenager, and I'll show you a miserable teenager. A teenager who refuses to try to understand why right is right is self-centered and self-serving. These two attributes always bring personal unhappiness.

3. Purity Protection

"But whoso committeth adultery with a woman lacketh understanding: he that doeth it destroyeth his own soul."—Prov. 6:32.

"Say unto wisdom, Thou art my sister; and call understanding thy kinswoman:

"That they may keep thee from the strange woman, from the stranger which flattereth with her words."—7:4, 5.

A teenager who begins to study the "why's" of the Bible will take to heart the biblical warnings and instruction concerning relationships with the opposite sex. He ceases to fight against the dating rules and curfews that his parents, in wisdom, have established, because he understands why they are needed.

4. Eliminates the Need for Punishment

"A rod is for the back of him that is void of understanding."—Prov. 10:13.

I am not just talking about parental punishment. Many adult Christians still refuse to become "men" in understanding. They don't want to understand why God wants them to do what He commands. They want to do what they want to do. Because of this immature attitude, they lead hard lives.

God knows how to push the right buttons. Because God loves us, He will chasten us when we act childish. Many times we, God's children, bring unnecessary

41

heartache and trials into our lives because we refuse to develop a biblical, eternal perspective on life.

5. A Passion for Life

"Understanding is a wellspring of life unto him that hath it."—Prov. 16:22.

Understanding the "why's" of the Christian life provides the passion for service. It transforms duty into delight. It directs service from the heart instead of just the mind. The effort to think like Christ is rewarded! When we share His thoughts, we also experience His passion. Understanding is the reason some Christians are filled with genuine joy. It is the emotion of service. It is not shallow. It is the icing on the cake of knowledge and wisdom.

6. Deepens Our Ability to Love God

"And the scribe said unto him, Well, Master, thou hast said the truth: for there is one God; and there is none other but he:

"And to love him with all the heart, and with all the understanding, and with all the soul, and with all the strength, and to love his neighbour as himself, is more than all whole burnt-offerings and sacrifices."—Mark 12:32, 33.

Taking the time to think through the doctrines of the Bible will deepen your appreciation and love for all that God has done. You cannot love the Lord "with all the understanding" if you remain immature in your understanding. Maturity loves at a higher level than immaturity. As you develop your understanding, you will increase in maturity. This will increase your capacity to love the Lord.

42

Discipline Your Thinking

The third aspect of maturity involves our thinking. Paul wrote, "When I was a child...I thought as a child." When he became a man, he "put away" immature thinking. He began to think like a man instead of a boy.

Does the Bible give us instruction concerning the maturity of our thinking? What is the difference between the way a child thinks and the way a man thinks? In Paul's instruction to Titus, he encourages the young preacher to exhort the young men to think properly, to mature in their thinking: "Young men likewise exhort to be sober minded" (Titus 2:6).

A mature mind is a sober mind. *A sober mind in the Bible means a disciplined mind.* What Paul is saying in I Corinthians 13 is, 'When I was a child, my mind was undisciplined. Then when I became a man, I began to discipline my thinking.'

The mature mind is a disciplined mind. God commands us to control our thoughts, to discipline our minds, to think correctly.

"*Casting down imaginations, and every high thing that exalteth itself against the knowledge of God, and bringing into captivity every thought to the obedience of Christ.*"—II Cor. 10:5.

Maturity is correcting and disciplining our thinking, capturing every sinful, evil or unproductive thought and banishing it from our minds. It is making our minds obey Christ. This is the challenge of teenage years.

Which kinds of thoughts should not be allowed in a mature, disciplined mind?

Daydreaming Versus Diligent Thoughts

"*I hate vain thoughts: but thy law do I love.*"—Ps. 119:113.

43

The word "vain" means desolate or empty. It is unproductive thinking.

King David, a man after God's own heart, said that he hated empty thoughts. It made him mad when he caught himself daydreaming. He did not make excuses for it but treated it as a weakness of character.

Nothing is as undisciplined and unproductive as a wandering mind. David realized that a healthy, intelligent mind was a gift from God, a gift to be used to accomplish things for God.

Children daydream. In our Christian school, I often walk by a desk and observe an elementary student just staring off into space, completely lost in another world. In front of him sits his unfinished assignment. He is wasting time and accomplishing nothing.

I clear my throat and bring him back to the here and now. He glances at me sheepishly and once again dives into his work. I smile to myself. Daydreaming is part of childhood, a characteristic of immaturity.

A mark of maturity is the ability to concentrate fully on a project until it is complete. The ability to focus is a valuable commodity in the workplace and one of the characteristics of a productive employee. In school, discipline, more than intellect, is the difference between the A and B students.

"The thoughts of the diligent tend only to plenteousness."—Prov. 21:5.

"Diligent thinking" is the opposite of "daydreaming." Diligent people use their minds to create and produce; they are always planning, evaluating or meditating. They discipline their minds to work, not wander. It is the kind of thinking that separates the mediocre businessman from the truly successful one, the kind of thinking that enables one man to get twice as much done in a week as the man who is undisciplined.

The Humble Mind Versus the Proud Mind

I registered as a freshman in college when I was seventeen years of age. One of my first-semester Bible classes was taught by a godly professor, Dr. Carl Laurent. On the very first day in his class he gave us an unusual assignment. We were required to look up and write down all of the verses in the Book of Proverbs that contained any form of the word "pride." The assignment was due the next day.

I rushed to my dormitory after class to begin my assignment and quickly finished it. The next day Dr. Laurent stood before the class and challenged us to stand and read any verse that we had found in which God had anything good to say about pride. No one stood. I reread the verses before me and found just the opposite was true. God hates pride. As a young man, it was one of the most valuable lessons I was ever taught.

"Put on therefore, as the elect of God, holy and beloved, bowels of mercies, kindness, humbleness of mind, meekness, longsuffering."—Col. 3:12.

"Let nothing be done through strife or vainglory; but in lowliness of mind let each esteem other better than themselves."—Phil. 2:3.

"Let this mind be in you, which was also in Christ Jesus:

"Who, being in the form of God, thought it not robbery to be equal with God:

"But made himself of no reputation, and took upon him the form of a servant, and was made in the likeness of men:

45

"And being found in fashion as a man, he humbled himself, and became obedient unto death, even the death of the cross."—Phil. 2:5–8.

One of the weaknesses of youth is pride. Dr. Laurent, recognizing this, did the incoming freshman class a favor by impressing upon our minds God's view of this sin. Anytime we think of ourselves more highly than we ought, we should immediately confess this sin to God, personally rebuke ourselves, and banish such thinking from our minds.

"For I say, through the grace given unto me, to every man that is among you, not to think of himself more highly than he ought to think; but to think soberly, according as God hath dealt to every man the measure of faith."—Rom. 12:3.

Sober or disciplined thinking refuses to allow men or women to think more highly of themselves than they ought. We ought to think of ourselves as children of God, because we are. We should think of ourselves as joint heirs of Christ, as overcomers, as beloved of God; because we are all these. But remember, these things are given to us by God. The moment we take credit for what we are or what we have accomplished, we commit the sin of pride.

The proud teenager says, "I can do all things." The humble teenager says, "I can do all things *through Christ* which strengtheneth me."

Evil Thinking Versus a Pure Mind

"Finally, brethren, whatsoever things are true, whatsoever things are honest, whatsoever things are just, whatsoever things are pure, whatsoever things are lovely, whatsoever things are of good report; if there be any virtue, and if there be any praise, think on these things."—Phil. 4:8.

46

The Devil will try to convince you that it is impossible to have a pure mind in this day and age. This is one of his lies. The commands of God are accompanied by the grace of God to carry them out. Nowhere is a disciplined mind more necessary than in the battle against wicked thoughts. Consider these Bible principles:

1. God knows our thoughts.

"O LORD, thou hast searched me, and known me.

"Thou knowest my downsitting and mine uprising, thou understandest my thought afar off."—Ps. 139:1, 2.

2. Wicked thoughts are an abomination unto the Lord.

"The thoughts of the wicked are an abomination to the Lord."—Prov. 15:26.

3. Wicked thoughts grieve the heart of our Lord.

"And God saw that the wickedness of man was great in the earth, and that every imagination of the thoughts of his heart was only evil continually.

"And it repented the LORD that he had made man on the earth, and it grieved him at his heart."—Gen. 6:5, 6.

In counseling young men who are frustrated because of their lack of victory over wicked thinking, I always share the above truths with them. Most already know all three. These truths will not give you victory over wicked thoughts, but they ought to give you the desire to have the victory. You must care about what God thinks and how He feels. Christ's question to Peter, His backslidden disciple, rings across the span of time: "Lovest thou me more than these?" Well? How about it, young person? Christ awaits your answer.

The secret to overcoming wicked thinking is to learn the scriptural practice of meditation.

The Power of Bible Meditation

"Be not overcome of evil, but overcome evil with good."—Rom. 12:21.

Every teenager needs to have Psalm 1 committed to memory. Read carefully the first three verses:

"Blessed is the man that walketh not in the counsel of the ungodly, nor standeth in the way of sinners, nor sitteth in the seat of the scornful.

"But his delight is in the law of the LORD; and in his law doth he meditate day and night.

"And he shall be like a tree planted by the rivers of water, that bringeth forth his fruit in his season; his leaf also shall not wither; and whatsoever he doeth shall prosper."—Ps. 1:1–3.

Let me describe most Christian teenagers that I meet today. Spiritually, they are like a tree planted in the desert—producing little or no spiritual fruit. They are spiritually *withered*—no spiritual energy, no passion, no victory. Why is this true? *No meditation!*

The Bible commands us to meditate upon three subjects:

1. The Person of God

"I will sing unto the LORD as long as I live: I will sing praise to my God while I have my being.

"My meditation of him shall be sweet: I will be glad in the LORD."—Ps. 104:33, 34.

2. The Works of God

"I will remember the works of the LORD: surely I will remember thy wonders of old.

"I will meditate also of all thy work, and talk of all thy doings."—Ps. 77:11, 12.

48

3. The Word of God

> *"O how love I thy law! it is my meditation all the day."*—Ps. 119:97.

We must be disciplined to think upon these things when wicked thoughts enter our minds. Good is stronger than evil. Overcome evil with good. A mature Christian learns to meditate on the character and Person of God. Start by writing down all the different titles God gives Himself. Why is He known by these things? Think! Meditate!

Next, write down a list of the mighty works of God— Bible stories that tell of His great miracles: the dividing of the Red Sea; manna from Heaven; turning water into wine; blind men given sight. Read one of these stories each morning, then meditate upon it all day long. What about the works of God in your own life?

Finally, we are commanded to meditate on the Word of God. As a teenager, I developed the habit of writing a verse of Scripture on a 3x5 card and carrying it with me. My goal was to memorize a verse a day. What I found out was that this single verse was also my greatest protection against the "fiery darts" of wicked thoughts that Satan hurled at me each day. I cannot begin to explain how this began to change me.

Any young person who makes the decision to begin to live like Christ, to think like Christ, will face the battle of his life.

> *"I find then a law, that, when I would do good, evil is present with me."*—Rom. 7:21.

If, after reading this book, you decide to accept the ultimate challenge of living like Christ, do not think that this decision will go unnoticed by Satan. For many of my teen years, I lived a defeated Christian life. I was saved and faithfully attended church, but in my personal Christian life I was a failure—a failure in my walk with God, in personal holiness, in my ability to stand for Christ, and especially in my thought life. I grew more and more disgusted with myself. Down deep I wanted to please the Lord, but I just couldn't seem to transfer that desire into action.

"For the good that I would I do not: but the evil which I would not, that I do."—Rom. 7:19.

For a few years, that could have been my life's verse. Many times I went to an altar to make the decision to do right but over the course of the next few days would again find myself floundering in defeat. I knew that the battle was being lost in my thought life.

Disgusted and tired of living a lie, I sat down one day and made five adjustments that changed my life.

1. I decided that I would make Christlikeness the ultimate goal of my life. I would never again settle for anything less.

2. I set my alarm clock an hour earlier each morning to study my Bible and pray.

3. I left the house each morning armed with a Scripture and a song. I would write down a verse on a 3x5 card and memorize it and meditate upon it during the day. I would then pick a song out of our hymnbook to sing throughout the day. With these, I would do battle with Satan over my thought life.

4. I disconnected the radio in my car. You will never have victory over wicked thoughts while listening to the wrong kind of music.

5. I dissolved several relationships. When I was

around certain people, it seemed almost impossible to do what was right. I am not blaming them; but for me to do what was right, these relationships had to be dissolved.

Of these five decisions, the single most helpful one was the decision to carry around a portion of God's Word. This was my defense against the constant attack on my mind.

You do not have to walk around as a defeated Christian! Saturate your mind with the Scriptures! Plant your mind by the rivers of water. Discipline yourself to meditate on the Word of God.

During His teenage years, Jesus increased in stature. He matured. In order to become like Jesus, put away childish things. Develop excellent speech. Deepen your biblical understanding. Discipline your thinking.

4

The Teenage Christ Increased in Favor With God

"And Jesus increased in wisdom and stature, and in favour with God and man."—Luke 2:52.

Jesus increased in favor with God? Why was this necessary? After all, this was the preexistent Son of God. Was He not already in favor with His Father?

Seldom do we think of all that was risked when Jesus agreed to become flesh, to become a man. He came as an infant, born of a virgin. He was faced with the trials of childhood and the challenges of the teenage years.

The above verse teaches us that Jesus was required by God to learn, to grow, to increase, just as is required of us. He did so without ever sinning. By His decisions and actions as a teenager, He increased in favor with God. Not just because of who He was, but because of what He did.

Peter, in his sermon to the house of Cornelius, makes this discovery about God:

"Of a truth I perceive that God is no respecter of persons:

"But in every nation he that feareth him, and worketh righteousness, is accepted with him."—Acts 10:34, 35.

God doesn't play favorites. He doesn't decide that

He just likes some people better than others. He does show favor to some and withholds His favor from others. this is not based on who they are but on what they do. In His Word, He specifically outlines the attributes and actions that cause a man to gain favor with Him.

How to Gain Favor With God

1. Righteousness secures the favor of God.

"For thou, LORD, wilt bless the righteous; with favour wilt thou compass him as with a shield."—Ps. 5:12.

"Fools make a mock at sin: but among the righteous there is favour."—Prov. 14:9.

Unlike man's favor, the favor of God is not based on appearance, education or financial standing. God is interested in righteousness. God is first an inspector of the heart, then of our actions. The righteousness that secures His favor is twofold: *positional* righteousness and *practical* righteousness.

Positional righteousness is how each of us stands before God in relation to His Son. As God looks into your heart, does He see that you have received the gift of eternal life made possible through His Son's death? Have you, by faith, chosen to believe and accept that Jesus died on the cross for your sins, was buried, and three days later arose from the dead? Are you born again? If so, positionally you stand before God made righteous by the blood of Christ.

This is extremely important, my young friend. If you have never been saved, you need to stop right where you are and admit to God that you are a sinner in need of salvation. Then ask Him for the gift of eternal life that was made available to you when Christ took your punishment and died for your sins on the cross. Sinner, will you right now pray this prayer and receive Jesus Christ as your personal Saviour?

Dear Lord, I know that I am a sinner and that the punishment for sin is eternal death. Thank You for sending Jesus to die on the cross for my sins. I believe that Jesus is the Son of God, that He did die for me, was buried, and three days later rose from the dead. Please give me your gift of eternal life. I do this moment choose to trust in Jesus as my personal Saviour and only hope for Heaven. Thank You for saving my soul. Amen.

"Whosoever shall call upon the name of the Lord shall be saved."—Rom. 10:13.

After God looks at our positional righteousness, He then looks at our practical righteousness—the everyday actions and thoughts of every true believer. God shows favor to those who strive to do right in every situation. Remember, *right* is defined by God's Word and not by our opinion.

Too many times Christians mimic the Israelites during their worst years when "every man did that which was right in his own eyes" (Judg. 17:6). Practical righteousness is striving to obey the commands and precepts of God's Word in our everyday life. With our striving will come success and failure. Practical righteousness gives God the glory when we succeed and seeks God's forgiveness when we fail. Striving, succeeding, failing, seeking His forgiveness and striving again—this is the pattern of the child of God who receives His favor.

2. The pursuit of wisdom secures the favor of God.

Any person who seeks the wisdom of God will secure His favor. Wisdom is personified in chapter 8 of Proverbs. It is given a divine personality and allowed to write that chapter.

"For whoso findeth me findeth life, and shall obtain favour of the LORD."—Prov. 8:35.

Let me repeat what we learned in the first chapter of this book: The pursuit of wisdom needs to be the principal priority of your teenage years. It was the first listed priority of the teenage Christ. It is identified in the Book of Proverbs as "the principal thing" for a young person to attain. When God sees a teenager decide to make the pursuit of wisdom a priority of his life, He responds by pouring out His favor upon him.

3. The performing of good works secures the favor of God.

"He that diligently seeketh good procureth favour: but he that seeketh mischief, it shall come unto him."—Prov. 11:27.

"A good man obtaineth favour of the LORD: but a man of wicked devices will he condemn."—12:2.

Salvation is a gift of God. It is "not of works, lest any man should boast." However, once we are saved, God expects us diligently to seek opportunities to do good. His favor is bestowed upon those who do.

We need an old-fashioned revival of kindness, of being a good neighbor. God smiles on those who are always looking for someone to help. He remembers those who remember the widows and fatherless. He rewards those who take time to encourage those around them.

So if you want the favor of God, then die to self and begin to live for others.

4. Finding a godly wife will secure the favor of God.

"Whoso findeth a wife findeth a good thing, and obtaineth favour of the LORD."—Prov. 18:22.

Obviously, it was not in the will of God for Jesus to marry. Securing the redemption of man was His passion. His completion was found in His mission. Occasionally, like Jesus, a young person will discover—over time—that it is not the will of God for him to marry. Like Paul, that person will be given the gift to be celibate. The Lord will give him a ministry that is so unique and important that it will require his full energy, passion and focus. In the work of God and in the person of the Lord Jesus he will find complete fulfillment (I Cor. 7:33–36).

However, for the vast majority of young people, it is the perfect will of God that they someday marry. It is important that a teenager establish very specific Bible principles concerning romantic relationships to safeguard against moral tragedy. More good young people have fallen out of favor with God because of wrong relationships with the opposite sex than for any other reason. Satan is good at exploiting the weakness of *youthful lusts*. The most important decision that you will make on earth, outside of salvation, is your choice of a marriage partner. It will determine to a large degree your direction and happiness.

If you feel that it is within the perfect will of God that you someday marry, consider carefully these verses found in chapter 2 of Genesis and the Bible principles that follow:

"*The LORD...brought her unto the man.*"—Vs. 22.

It is perfectly natural for a young person to have a secret desire to be happily married someday. You may not talk about it, but it is there. You may never admit it to your friends, but when you are alone, you dream about it.

There is a couple in your church whom you secretly watch. They obviously have a close marriage. During public prayer, you peek (young people are great peekers!). You watch the man slip his hand into his wife's as they pray together. You watch them talk and see the love communicated through their eyes. You see the gentleness that the husband uses when he is with her. You think within yourself, *Is there someone like that out there for me?* The desire someday to be happily married is a divine desire. God put it there. He understood that it was not good for man to be alone.

God has created someone specifically for you. Eve was created as the perfect fit, the perfect complement to Adam. God did not create six women, then say to Adam when he awoke, "Date each of these and choose the one you like the best!" He made one woman specifically for him. You must believe that there is someone who has been created just for you.

A part of you is in that specific one created for you. Eve had a part of Adam inside of her. God took a piece of Adam, a rib, and placed it inside of Eve. I believe God has done the same for every young person whom He created with marriage as a part of His perfect will for him. Someone out there has a part of you in him/her.

If it is God's will for you to marry someday, you will never feel complete until you meet this person. The greatest mystery of marriage is this: how can two people become one flesh? Yet God states that when two people are married, they do become one. They become one because each is incomplete without the other. The divine longing that you feel is a desire to be whole.

God will bring that person to you. God did not come to Adam after he awoke and say, "Okay, I created someone for you and hid her somewhere in the garden. Good luck finding her!" In His time, He brought the one made for Adam to him.

There is a great deal of pressure on young people to have a boyfriend or girlfriend. Many young people have tied their self-worth to these relationships. They have been led to believe that there is something wrong with them if they are not involved with someone.

The result of this thinking is tragic. Relationships not sanctioned by God have resulted in the theft of the purity of many Christian teens.

Be patient and wait for God to bring you His perfect will in His time.

Adam had to stay in the garden in order to meet Eve. Don't miss this! If you choose to leave the perfect will of God, you sacrifice meeting the one God has created for you. This meeting will occur along the path of God's will.

So keep yourself pure. Save yourself for the special one God has for you. How serious it is to backslide! How serious it is to choose what you want to do with your life instead of asking God what He wants you to do!

Your teenage years should be about preparing for marriage. Begin now to prepare for that special one God will someday give you. Begin to pray for that person even though you don't yet know for sure who it is. Young ladies, begin now to learn the skills that will make you a great homemaker. Gentlemen, begin now to prepare to be a good provider.

Most young people today spend the bulk of their youth involved in activities that will do nothing to prepare them for real life. The teenage years should not be about playing but about preparing; not about pursuing but about patience. God gives His best to those who are willing to wait!

Trusting the Lord, patiently waiting for His time and staying in His will are the characteristics of the young person who lives in the light of God's favor.

5. Do a word study on these two words: *blessed* and *cursed*.

One of the most profitable Bible studies I have ever done was a word study of the various forms of two Bible words: *blessed* and *cursed*.

The Lord challenged me to do this study while I was studying the life of King David. I read in the Bible that David was a man after God's own heart. I watched as God blessed him time and time again, and found myself becoming envious of the sweet relationship that they seemed to enjoy. I remember thinking to myself, *Wouldn't it be great to receive the favor and blessings that God seemed to shower upon David? It must be nice to be one of God's favorites.*

The Holy Spirit quickly brought to mind two verses that I had read just weeks before:

> *"Then Peter opened his mouth, and said, Of a truth I perceive that God is no respecter of persons:*
> *"But in every nation he that feareth him, and worketh righteousness, is accepted with him."*—Acts 10:34, 35.

As I meditated on these verses, I was reminded of several truths:

1. God is no respecter of persons. He does not play favorites.

2. God is honorable and keeps His word. He has never lied or gone back on a promise.

3. The Bible is the Word of God. Every verse has

been inspired and preserved by Him personally.

4. In the Bible, He has outlined what actions and attitudes will result in His blessing.

5. In the Bible, He has also outlined what actions and attitudes will result in a curse.

6. If I carefully study every form of the word blessed and compile a list of all those things that bring about God's blessing—and do them—God will keep His word and bless me and my family. And if I do the same with every form of the word *cursed* and avoid doing those things that bring about the curse of God upon a life, I won't have to suffer needlessly.

So I did, and you can too.

6. Study the lives of Bible heroes who found favor with God.

Abraham, Moses, Joshua, Joseph, Ruth, Esther—the list goes on and on. Let me suggest a starting place. Although it is obvious that many Bible heroes secured the favor of God, the Bible only specifically used the phrase 'found favor with God' with four individuals.

a. *Young ladies, study the life of Mary, Christ's mother.* Gabriel greets her in Luke, chapter 1, with this proclamation, "Hail, thou that art highly favoured, the Lord is with thee"! Every young lady should want to find out why. Study Mary's life. Find every verse that mentions her. Study every story in which she is mentioned.

b. *Young men, study the life of David.* In Stephen's sermon in Acts, chapter 7, David is identified as a man "who found favour before God." In I Samuel, chapter 13, he is described as a man after God's own heart. Study the character of David. Even in failure, he did what was necessary to obtain the favor of God again.

Remember, God is no respecter of persons. If we possess the characteristics that endeared David to God's heart, we too can gain His favor.

c. *Study the life of Samuel.* Samuel alone shares with Christ the distinction of a man "in favour both with the LORD, and also with men" (I Sam. 2:26). What is even more amazing is that, like Christ, Samuel received this compliment while he was still a young man. What a fascinating teenager! Much can be gleaned from a study of the life of Samuel.

d. *Study our supreme example, the Lord Jesus Christ.* Every teenager should spend a great deal of time reading and studying the Gospels. God has penned down four books—Matthew, Mark, Luke and John—which allow us to walk beside Jesus as He walked upon this earth. Make yourself the thirteenth disciple. As you read the Gospels, picture every story in your mind. Watch everything that Jesus does, then ask yourself, *Why did He do that?* Listen to everything that He says, then ask, *To whom was He talking? Why did He say that, and what did He mean?* Examine every decision that He makes, then ask, *Why?* Nothing that He did was by accident. Nothing that He did was unimportant.

The ultimate goal of the Christian life is to be like Jesus. God the Father spoke from Heaven with an audible voice to show His approval of His Son: "This is my beloved Son, in whom I am well pleased" (Matt. 3:17).

When we mimic Christ in attitude and action, we secure the favor of God.

5

The Teenage Christ Increased in Favor With Man

"And Jesus increased in wisdom and stature, and in favour with God and man."—Luke 2:52.

As a teenager, Jesus grew in favor with man. He was wise enough to gain the respect of the adults of His village. He conducted Himself in such a manner as to gain the admiration of His peers. The word "favour" in this verse comes from a root word which means "to cheer." People around Him were cheered by His presence. His attitude refreshed them. His greetings encouraged them. His character and wisdom challenged them to be their best.

I believe teenagers have been given the impression that you cannot gain favor with God without falling out of favor with man. I have found that although the world will not always understand or agree with our scriptural conduct and convictions, most of the time that is not what causes us to lose favor with men. Often our *disposition* turns people off, not our *position*. A Christian teenager can gain the respect of adults and the admiration of his peers and still grow in favor with his God.

It Matters What Adults Think of You!

I watch the actions of young people when they are

63

The Teenage Years of Jesus Christ

around adults. I watch the *reactions* of adults when they are around teenagers. Most teenagers today seem to care little about what adults think about them. They are so busy trying to impress their peers that they are oblivious to the opinions of anyone more than a few years older than they are.

This is not how Christ lived. Men respected Him. Adults were impressed by Him.

Why was this important? Why is it important today that you live in a way that gains the respect of adults?

Your parents are adults. You have not been instructed in the Bible to obey your peers. You have not been instructed in the Bible to honor your peers. You have not been promised prosperity, peace and long life if you please your peers.

The most dangerous time in a young person's life is when he begins to value the opinion of his friends more than the opinion of his parents.

Your pastor is an adult. He is the watchman on the wall. He is the one who watches for your soul. You are commanded by God to remember him. You are commanded to follow his faith, to consider the end of his conversation (Heb. 13:7, 17). You are instructed to obey his biblical instruction, to submit to his leadership as he guides your local church.

Again, a teenager is in grave spiritual danger when he begins to exalt the counsel of his peers above the counsel of his pastor.

Your teachers are adults. Satan has worked very hard to propagate the lie of the '60s: "Never trust anyone over thirty." Yet in Titus, chapter 2, God instructs the younger women to learn from the elder women and the younger men to learn from the previous genera-

64

tion. Your attitude toward adults will determine your attitude toward godly instruction.

Your boss will be an adult. Your peers will not hire you. An adult's impression of you will determine whether or not you receive a good job—and whether you keep it! The rebels are the ones who spend their lives complaining that they cannot find a good job. Adult employers are not impressed by immaturity and irresponsibility, nor will they tolerate it for very long.

You will never achieve Christlikeness until you learn to gain the respect of adults. This is the ultimate goal and the ultimate reason.

The teenage Christ lived in such a way that He gained the admiration and respect of those over Him. He did so without compromising the favor of God. You can too! But first you must discover what attributes gain the respect of adults.

Character Traits Adults Respect in Teenagers

"Let no man despise thy youth; but be thou an example of the believers, in word, in conversation, in charity, in spirit, in faith, in purity."—I Tim. 4:12.

You say, "Adults are not supposed to despise my youth! The Bible says so!"

Read the verse again. It is not written to correct the attitude of adults toward teenagers but written to the young and contains instruction on how to live so you will not be held in low esteem because of your age. It puts the burden on you, not them: "...but *be thou....*"

Right now you have a reputation among the adults who know you and work with you. Proverbs 20:11 tells us, "Even a child is known by his doings." Adults watch young people. You are being watched even when you think no one is paying attention. Adults base their assessment of you by examining six areas of your life. In these six areas, you are commanded by God to be an example of what a believer is supposed to be.

1. Adults respect excellent speech. Words are a window to your soul, a result of the abundance of your heart, and the revealing of who you really are. Adults know this, and they listen.

I encourage you to review "The Ten Laws of Excellent Speech" found in chapter 3. Memorize them. Meditate upon them. Carry a copy of them around on a 3x5 card and review them until they become engraved upon your heart. What you say does matter!

2. Adults respect mature behavior. "Conversation" in I Timothy 4:12 speaks of your conduct. It is the "doings" by which you are known. Is your behavior appropriate to the situation? How do you behave during church? How about before and after church? Basic manners are important and make a big impression.

Learn to exercise common courtesy. Greet people warmly and sincerely. Young men, be gentlemen. Young ladies, carry yourselves with grace and dignity.

3. Adults respect selfless love. God says in His Word that in the last days men will be lovers of their own selves. A selfish, self-centered teenager is contemptible in the eyes of an adult. However, a young person who is openly affectionate toward his parents, grandparents and siblings is greatly admired. Also, your love for God and the things of God should be obvious for all to see.

4. Adults respect a good attitude. One man said, "Your attitude, not your aptitude, determines your alti-

tude!" Another said, "Your attitude reveals your gratitude." A good attitude is admired and appreciated by
everyone.

Learn to be enthusiastic! Don't grumble when everything isn't going your way. Start counting your blessings instead of pouting! Nothing screams immaturity
more than a negative attitude.

5. Adults respect sincere faith. How refreshing to
see young people serving God! What an encouragement to see a teenager read his Bible, pray and witness
for Christ! I love to see teens singing specials in the
church, joining in during testimony time, and openly
and unashamedly standing up for their Lord. You gain
the respect and rejoice the heart of adults when you
are willing to display your faith in God.

6. Adults respect wholesome purity. The Bible
instructs you, "Flee...youthful lusts." People watch how
you interact with the opposite sex. They watch your
eyes. A young person who is undisciplined in his or her
desires will not be respected.

Gentlemen, train yourself to avoid looking at inap-
propriate advertisements. When you look at a lady,
look her in the eye. Keep hands off. Never speak sug-
gestively. Beware of the world's perverse brand of
humor. Be an example of the believer in purity.

Young ladies, dress modestly and appropriately.
Tight-fitting clothes do not make you look sexy; they
make you look *cheap*. Don't be a flirt! Keep hands off.
Be especially appropriate around married men. *No one
respects a girl with loose morals.* Wicked men may give
you attention, then use you, but they won't marry you.
Be an example of the believer in purity.

The goal of every Christian teenager should be to

arrive at the marriage altar pure and chaste. If you do not, you lose a degree of credibility that you never fully regain.

As Jesus increased in favor with God, He also gained the respect of every adult in Nazareth by being an example of the believer—in word, in behavior, in love, in attitude, in faith and in purity.

How to Respond to the Reaction of Your Peers

"For he shall grow up before him as a tender plant, and as a root out of a dry ground: he hath no form nor comeliness: and when we shall see him, there is no beauty that we should desire him.

"He is despised and rejected of men; a man of sorrows, and acquainted with grief: and we hid as it were our faces from him; he was despised, and we esteemed him not."—Isa. 53:2, 3.

Every young person who has ever decided to make Christlikeness the goal of his life has had to deal with some degree of negative response from his peers. Immaturity has never embraced maturity. Carnality has never rejoiced at the presence of someone spiritual. Foolishness has always tried to ostracize those who have made wisdom the principal goal of their lives. Men in darkness hate light.

I wish I could say that if you decide to put into practice the principles found in this book, you will be popular, but you won't. Even within a Christian school or a good Bible-believing church, you will often be misunderstood.

Congratulations! Welcome to the club!

The teenage Christ was often misunderstood, often despised. Sorrow was a close friend; grief, a well-known acquaintance. Many of His own age group turned their backs on Him. It will be no different for you.

Learn now that you cannot live to please your peers. Their reaction is an attempt to make you become like them, to control you. Seldom will you be able to gain the favor of God and adults and also gain the favor of your own age group. You cannot control how they react to you, but you must control your reaction to them.

1. Be friendly to everyone, but choose your friends wisely. Decide that you will walk with wise men. One godly friend is worth more than all of the carnal crowd put together.

2. Embrace solitude. It is the training ground of greatness. Moses came from the backside of the desert to lead the children of Israel. Gideon was alone threshing wheat when God called him to judge Israel. David had to be sent for so that he could be anointed king of Israel; he was out alone on the hills of Judea tending the sheep. Elijah and Elisha were both loners. John the Baptist was raised in the wilderness, an oddball and an outcast.

You will never accomplish great things if you never have great thoughts. Great thoughts are afraid of crowds. They seek out the one who is alone, seeking them.

3. Forget popularity. Too often popularity and principles cannot coexist. Never forsake Bible principles for popularity. Forget popularity! Be satisfied with respect.

4. Never defend yourself when criticized. Defend your family, your friends, the weak, but never defend yourself. A pure life is your best defense.

5. Don't be a Pharisee. Pride taints a man's piety. Never allow yourself the luxury of comparing yourself with others. Only comparing yourself with Christ will keep you humble.

6. Avoid the cliques. Befriend the friendless. Never count how many people are a friend to you. Only be concerned with how many people you can befriend.

7. Be yourself. Learn from others, but be you.

8. Overcome evil with good. Return an act of kindness for every evil intent. Pray for them who despitefully use you. Good is stronger! Never lower yourself to respond to evil with evil.

9. Apologize when wrong. Everyone respects someone who is quick to apologize when he is wrong. Crow is best eaten when fresh.

10. Smile. It drives them nuts!

6

The Teenage Christ Remained Subject to His Parents

"And he [Jesus] went down with them, and came to Nazareth, and was subject unto them."—Luke 2:51.

Except for your relationship with God, your relationship to your parents is the most important relationship of your teenage years.

Satan works feverishly to destroy this relationship. He is the original rebel. As one of God's exalted angels, he refused to submit to the authority of God. Ever since, he has carried his work of rebellion into the homes of this world.

Jesus, who deserves to be exalted, humbled Himself to the will of His heavenly Father and His earthly parents. Imagine, the God-Man subject unto men; the Creator subject to His creation; sinlessness submitting to imperfect leadership! He expects no less from us.

Every teenager will choose to follow one of these two examples.

The difference between Christ and Satan in the area of submission is simple. Satan made the foolish conclusion that rebellion would lead to superiority. Christ, who is the wisdom of God, understood that superiority is a result of submission.

71

The Superiority of Submission

Your relationship toward your parents will affect every other relationship of your life. Submissive teenagers make superior adults. A teenager who refuses to place himself under the authority of his parents will struggle in every area of his adult life.

1. A submissive teenager becomes a superior citizen.

"Submit yourselves to every ordinance of man for the Lord's sake."—I Pet. 2:13.

"Let every soul be subject unto the higher powers. For there is no power but of God: the powers that be are ordained of God."—Rom. 13:1.

The home is the training ground for society. Communities all over America are trying to find a solution to the problem of juvenile crime. These problems are being created in the home. Our prisons are full of men and women who, when young, would not submit to the rules of their parents and, as a result, refused to submit to the laws of society.

2. A submissive teenager becomes a superior employee.

"Servants, be subject to your masters with all fear; not only to the good and gentle, but also to the froward."—I Pet. 2:18.

A great employee is one who cheerfully and completely follows the orders of those over him. He finds favor in the eyes of his employer and is promoted into positions of authority.

Many drift from job to job and cause their families unnecessary financial struggles simply because they never learned to obey. No one wants to pay good money to an arrogant and disobedient employee.

3. A submissive teenager becomes a superior church member.

*"Remember them which have the rule over you, who have spoken unto you the word of God: whose faith follow, considering the end of their conversation."—*Heb. 13:7.

*"Obey them that have the rule over you, and submit yourselves: for they watch for your souls."—*Vs. 17.

The apostle John was very straightforward when dealing with church troublemakers. In his letter to Gaius, he openly rebukes a man by the name of Diotrephes, who loved to have the preeminence in the church and thus refused to submit to the apostle John's leadership (III John). Diotrephes obviously didn't start insisting on having everything his way only after he became an adult.

A teenager who gives his parents grief will someday give a pastor grief. There is no such thing as selective rebellion. If you will not submit to your parents, you will grow up to be a selfish, strong-willed church member who will cause problems in the church you attend.

4. A submissive teenage girl becomes a superior wife.

*"Wives, submit yourselves unto your own husbands, as unto the Lord."—*Eph. 5:22.

I often tell the teenage boys in our youth group, "Gentlemen, if you become interested in a young lady, take a close look at her relationship with her parents. How does she treat her mom? Is she close to her father? Does she have a servant's heart? Stubbornness and rebellion are the traits of a practicing witch, not a potential wife" (I Sam. 15:23).

Occasionally, I will hear about a boy who broke up

with a young lady because he felt she wasn't submissive to him. Well, knucklehead, she isn't commanded to be submissive to you but to be submissive to her parents. I worry about any young man who tries to steal that position of authority from a girl's parents.

Young ladies, if you are involved with a guy like that, *drop him like a hot potato!* A wise young man will encourage his girlfriend or fiancée to love, honor and obey her parents. If she is submissive and loving to them, she will one day make him a fine wife.

5. A submissive teenage boy becomes a superior leader.

"And whosoever shall exalt himself shall be abased; and he that shall humble himself shall be exalted."— Matt. 23:12.

I have never met a great leader who was not first a great follower. "Followship" is a prerequisite of leadership. Every great Bible leader was once a faithful servant whom God plucked from obscurity and exalted to prominence. Jesus tried to explain this to His disciples when He overheard them arguing about who was greatest. He told them that the world judged greatness by a man's position and authority. In God's eyes, the servant is greatest.

A young man who seeks to lead will be destined to follow. The young man who seeks to follow qualifies himself as a possible leader. This "followship" is first developed in the home. A young man who feels that he has outgrown the need to obey his mother is weak and unqualified to lead. A young man who believes that manhood is obtained by rebelling against the authority of his father understands nothing about manhood or greatness.

Watch the young man who obeys his parents. Watch the young man who says "Yes sir" and "No sir." Watch the young man who respects his teachers and submits to their authority. That is the young man who will someday be exalted.

6. A submissive teenager becomes a superior Christian.

"Let this mind be in you, which was also in Christ Jesus:

"Who, being in the form of God, thought it not robbery to be equal with God:

"But made himself of no reputation, and took upon him the form of a servant, and was made in the likeness of men:

"And being found in fashion as a man, he humbled himself, and became obedient unto death, even the death of the cross."—Phil. 2:5–8.

The ultimate goal of the Christian life is to be like Jesus. The teenager who is not submissive to his parents is a lousy Christian. It matters not how many other spiritual accomplishments he can claim; if he fails in submission, he fails in the ultimate goal. Christ was God, yet He submitted Himself to the earthly authority of His parents. He expects no less from us.

Jesus was subject to both authority figures in the home, to both His natural mother and Joseph. It is worth pointing out that Joseph was not His biological father. Christ was the virgin-born Son of God. Yet Jesus respected Joseph's position and submitted to his authority as the head of the home.

Many young people today are being reared in homes where they have a stepfather or stepmother. Many believe that they do not have to obey them, because they are not their real parents. Christ, by His

75

personal example, has shown us that this is no excuse for rebellion. Jesus learned everything He could from Joseph, as we will see in the next chapter.

7

The Teenage Christ Learned a Wage-Earning Skill

"Is not this the carpenter's son? is not his mother called Mary?"—Matt. 13:55.

"Is not this the carpenter?"—Mark 6:3.

Before Jesus was a preacher, He was a carpenter. Before He ever healed the sick or raised the dead, He carefully crafted carts and cabinets. His hands were calloused. His biceps were knotted with the strength of hard labor. He rose up early and worked beside Joseph, learning the skills of a craftsman. These skills were mastered during His teenage years.

The Importance of Learning the Work Ethic

I'm tired of lazy teenagers—I'll tell you that from the beginning. I despise being in the presence of a lazy person. It causes me more genuine anger than you can possibly imagine. I also think it angers God.

I hear people say, "Let them have their teenage years. They are going to have to work their whole lives." I also have seen the result of that thinking.

I have watched a generation who were allowed to play instead of prepare, watch instead of work, and take instead of give. The product of this misguided and

77

unscriptural social experiment has been a generation of couch potatoes, spoiled brats and thankless vandals. The teenage Christ was none of these.

Before you assume that I am putting every young person in the same boat, please allow me to allow you the opportunity to redeem yourself. Below is a test. There are no trick questions. Each one requires a simple *yes* or *no* answer. The Bible will be used as the basis of determining whether you are diligent or slothful. (Perhaps you should allow your parents to help you answer these questions. ☺)

1. Do you often fail to take care of the things that have been provided for you?_____
2. Are you constantly asking your parents to buy you things?_____
3. Do you make excuses to get out of doing your work?_____
4. Is your bedroom generally untidy and unorganized?_____
5. Do you sleep more than is absolutely necessary?_____
6. Do you have to be reminded to do your simple daily chores?_____
7. Do you have a lot of idle time?_____
8. Do you work harder when a teacher is watching you?_____
9. Do you look for reasons to put off doing a job?_____
10. Were you too conceited to be absolutely honest in answering the above questions?_____

Are you finished? Were you completely honest?

Now, let's look at what the Word of God has to say about each of the above questions.

1. Do you often fail to take care of the things that have been provided for you?

"He also that is slothful in his work is brother to him that is a great waster."—Prov. 18:9.

Your bike is left out in the rain. Your clothes are crumpled in a ball on the floor. Game pieces are missing because they were not carefully put back after use. School clothes are ruined because you did not take time to change into proper play clothes after school. You are wasting that which has cost others time and money. Diligent teenagers properly care for the things that have been provided for them.

2. Are you constantly asking your parents to buy you things?

"The desire of the slothful killeth him; for his hands refuse to labour.

"He coveteth greedily all the day long."—Prov. 21:25, 26.

Why are you asking Mom and Dad to buy things for you? You say it is their job to provide for you. For how long? Why is it that able-bodied sixteen-year-olds are still having their parents buy their school clothes for them? Oh, I forgot. You are too busy with basketball, baseball, football and track to be expected to get a job. You are too busy *playing*.

If you want something, get a job, save your money, then buy it. You might find out that you won't want as much if you are the one buying it.

3. Do you make excuses to get out of doing your work?

"The slothful man saith, There is a lion without, I shall

be slain in the streets."—Prov. 22:13.

A lion in the streets? Excuses sound foolish to everyone except the one giving them. Someone once told me, "Excuses are like armpits. Everyone seems to have a couple, and they all stink!" I can't picture the teenage Christ making foolish excuses to His parents and teachers. Can you?

4. Is your bedroom generally untidy and unorganized?

"I went by the field of the slothful, and by the vineyard of the man void of understanding;

"And, lo, it was all grown over with thorns, and nettles had covered the face thereof, and the stone wall thereof was broken down."—Prov. 24:30, 31.

Disarray due to neglect. Neglect due to slothfulness. Your room is your responsibility. By the age of twelve, you should not only be responsible enough to keep your room clean, but you should also be helping your mother in other areas of the home.

5. Do you sleep more than is absolutely necessary?

"How long wilt thou sleep, O sluggard? when wilt thou arise out of thy sleep?

"Yet a little sleep, a little slumber, a little folding of the hands to sleep:

"So shall thy poverty come as one that travelleth, and thy want as an armed man."—Prov. 6:9–11.

Notice that the Bible points out that it just takes a little sleep, a little slumber. If you are sleeping, you are not producing. A person who decides to get by on just one less hour of sleep a night adds fifteen days of productivity to every year. Over the next fifty years, you will have two extra years of productivity. Two years! I've knocked on the door of teenagers at ten o'clock in the morning on a Saturday and have awaened them. Sluggard! Get out of bed and do something with your life!

6. Do you have to be reminded to do your simple daily chores?

"The slothful hideth his hand in his bosom; it grieveth him to bring it again to his mouth."—Prov. 26:15.

A lazy teenager resents being asked to do the simplest of tasks. Instead of jumping up to help serve, he expects others to serve him. He complains that his sister or brother should have to do a job instead of him.

I often try to imagine what a joy Jesus must have been to His parents with His helpful spirit and ready hands. I wonder how many times Mary had to remind Jesus to do His chores.

7. Do you have a lot of idle time?

"Slothfulness casteth into a deep sleep; and an idle soul shall suffer hunger."—Prov. 19:15.

Idle time is the result of an idle soul. An idle soul is unfulfilled. "I'm bored!" A spiritual teenager who is in tune with the Holy Spirit will always have something to do. There is so much good that can be done with your life, so many people whose lives you can touch. Idle time is most often filled with unproductive and unimaginative activities like video games and television.

8. Do you work harder when a teacher is watching you?

"Go to the ant, thou sluggard; consider her ways, and be wise:

"Which having no guide, overseer, or ruler,

"Provideth her meat in the summer, and gathereth her food in the harvest."—Prov. 6:6–8.

An insect works hard without any supervision. An insect. An insect!

9. Do you look for reasons to put off doing a job?

"The sluggard will not plow by reason of the cold; therefore shall he beg in harvest, and have nothing."— Prov. 20:4.

It's too cold today. I'll do it tomorrow. I'm too tired. It's too hot. It's too hard. It's not due till next week. I'll do it later.

10. Were you too conceited to be absolutely honest in answering the above questions?

*"The sluggard is wiser in his own conceit than seven men that can render a reason."—*Prov. 26:16.

Pride often keeps us from being honest with ourselves. Take the test again, now that you know what the Bible says. Ask the Holy Spirit to convict you and help you to overcome the slothfulness that is behind many of your bad habits. No man will succeed in his quest to be like Jesus until he begins to be brutally honest with himself about himself.

Now for fun, I'll let you score your own paper!

Yes	No	Score
0–2	8–10	You've been well trained. Keep it up.
3–4	6–7	You're on your way! Seek to improve!
5–6	4–5	You're probably average. But who wants to be average?
7–8	2–3	Target one or two areas and work on them this week.
9–10	0–1	At least you're honest. Now get to work!

The Importance of Mastering a Wage-Earning Skill

Joseph did not just teach "his" Son to work; he taught Him a trade, a trade that Jesus could use the rest of His life to earn a living. Most Bible teachers believe that Joseph died long before Jesus turned thirty years of age—that at least for a time, Jesus was the One who provided for the needs of His mother and His siblings. While on the cross, Jesus gave John the responsibility to care for Mary, His mother. The trade He mastered as a youth was useful in providing for the needs of His family.

Young man, prepare now to be a good provider. While you are a teenager, become an apprentice to someone who has a skilled trade. By the time you graduate from high school, you can be on your way to mastering a marketable skill. You will be leaps and bounds ahead of others your age. But first you must set a goal and have a plan. Consider the following suggestions:

Learn the skills that your father uses every day. A wise boy will watch his father carefully as he works on projects around the house. When Dad is fixing something, get in there and help! This will help you to learn basic home maintenance skills and develop common sense.

Learn the basics of your father's trade. If he possesses a marketable skill, ask him to train you in his area of expertise.

Recently a Christian came to our church to tune the piano. He said if I would bring the students of our Christian school up to the auditorium, he would take a few minutes to show them the inside of a piano and explain how it works. Feeling it would be a great experience for them, we took him up on his offer.

At the end of his presentation, he asked if there were any questions.

One of our young ladies asked, "How did you learn to tune a piano?"

His answer was amazing:

> My father was a musician and a piano tuner. He had a firm belief that I should be taught a trade before I left the house. So, when I was fifteen years old, he went around and bought forty old pianos, all in need of some repair.
>
> Over the next year, under his supervision, he had me take each one completely apart and rebuild it and tune it. He then sold those pianos and with the money sent me to a piano-tuning school so I could become even more proficient. I had other dreams and ambitions, but he said I could pursue them after I learned to tune pianos.
>
> Later in life, I returned to the trade my father had insisted that I learn; and for the last seventeen years, I have made my living tuning pianos.

He then went on to bless his father for seeing to it that he learned a wage-earning skill while he was still in his teenage years.

Make a list of the trades represented by the members of the church that you attend. Ask your pastor for a membership list and find out what the men do to make a living. Here is a partial list of the skilled labor in my home church:

carpet cleaner	printer	electrician
roofer	equipment salesman	farmer
machinist	diesel mechanic	welder
TV repairman	plumber	carpenter
carpet installer	mechanic	butcher

If you are between the ages of twelve and fourteen, ask these men to allow you to work with them occasionally so you can begin to learn from them. Be sure to get your parents to approve the people you will ask before you ask them. You must understand that these people are busy making a living for their families. Not all of them will be in a position to accommodate your request. Do not ask for a job. Do not expect to be paid. At this age, you should be grateful for the chance just to tag along and learn.

If you are between the ages of fifteen and eighteen and have learned the work ethic, ask these men if there is a chance to work for them during the summer. Again, get your parents' input first. Expect to work for a minimum, entry-level wage. You are still learning and are not worth a lot to them while you are being trained. They are doing you a favor for giving you on-the-job training.

As much as is possible, watch how they do what they do. Ask questions. Listen. Learn to anticipate their next move. Have the proper tools waiting for them before they have to ask for them. Remember, at this stage, it is not important how much you *earn* but how much you *learn*.

It is very important for Christian young people to work for Christian employers. Your character is still being formed during your teenage years. I have seen too many teenagers backslide after getting a job working for a worldly boss and with worldly teenagers. Do not take a job that will require you to miss any of your church services. Make this very plain to your employer, even if he is a Christian.

Work hard to master at least one wage-earning skill before you graduate from high school. Even if this is not what you end up doing for the rest of your life, it will always give you something to fall back on. It may be the job you will use to finance your way through college or later provide a second income on the side, if you ever find yourself in need of extra money.

A young man in our church left last fall to go to Bible college. During his last two years of high school, he worked for one of the men in our church who is a carpet installer. He worked hard, paid attention and learned. The man took the time to show this young man how to lay laminate flooring, and the young man practiced until he could do a good job on his own.

When he arrived at Bible college, he got a phone book, wrote down the addresses of floor covering stores in that area and began to visit them one by one. He would ask for the owner, introduce himself, then announce, "I can lay laminate flooring, and I need a job."

As you might imagine, most of these owners were pretty skeptical about the abilities of an eighteen-year-old kid. Most just smiled politely, took his phone number and said they would keep him in mind. He would then get in his car and go to the next one.

One of the last stores on his list was a small, family-owned business. He again introduced himself, then announced, "I can lay laminate flooring, and I need a job."

The owner smiled over at his wife, then looked at the young man and said, "Come with me." He took him to a corner of his showroom and pointed down to the bare, stripped floor. "I was just getting ready to install a laminate floor display area here. There is the flooring. Let's see what you can do."

The young man took off his jacket and went to work. Within a few hours the job was done.

"You *can* lay laminate flooring! I need someone to work for me part-time. When can you start?"

The young man shared this story with me when he came home for Christmas break. He also told me that on the previous Saturday he had helped his boss on a job that had taken him five hours and had earned him three hundred dollars. He was able to earn that much because while he was in junior high he had learned the work ethic and, while in high school, he had the dedication and wisdom to learn a wage-earning skill.

Young lady, prepare now to be a successful homemaker. Learn the skills that your mother uses every day of her life. The ability to make a house into a home is fast becoming a lost art. Learn from your mother and your grandmothers. Never apologize for spending your teenage years preparing to be a good wife and mother. There is no greater calling.

Learn the skills and character traits that will enable you to save your family money in the future.

Over the years of our marriage, my wife has saved us thousands of dollars by shopping smart, clipping coupons, sewing, creating meals from scratch, garage sale shopping, etc. Instead of charging an item, she saves up for it or puts it in layaway and pays on it a little at a time. This practice alone has saved us hundreds of dollars in interest over the years.

As a teenager, she was taught by her mother the qualities of thriftiness and contentment. She learned the skills that allow her to *create* instead of *buy*. She learned how to budget her money and balance her checkbook. It is my contention that she has saved me more money by doing these things than she could ever have earned by joining the work force.

Learn a skill that will enable you to become a stay-at-home entrepreneur. The virtuous lady of Proverbs 31 made her family and home the priority of her life. In addition, she developed skills that enabled her to contribute financially.

"She considereth a field, and buyeth it: with the fruit of her hands she planteth a vineyard."

"She maketh fine linen and selleth it; and delivereth girdles unto the merchant."—Prov. 31:16, 24.

Obviously, she did not make as much as her husband, whose job was to provide for his family. She is not expected to, because her God-given priority is different. However, I believe that you can and should develop skills that you can use in the home to provide you with additional income.

Now more than ever there are great opportunities for a lady to hold down a part-time job from her own home. Talk to the ladies of your church and glean ideas from them.

Develop skills and abilities that will make you an asset to your local church. Ladies have constituted the great army of volunteers who have helped make churches successful for generations. The desire for the temporal rewards of a career over the eternal rewards of service to family and God has greatly depleted this great resource.

During your teenage years, learn to serve in your local church. Music should be a part of young ladies' priorities. Most of all, develop a servant's heart, a heart willing to do whatever will make the work of God go forward.

Nothing is more exciting than to watch God bring together a young man who has spent his teen years preparing to be what God has created him to be and a young lady who is polished and prepared to be a successful wife and mother. *What a dynamic duo!* This is the couple whose lives will be used greatly for God's glory.

8
Putting It All Together

"But be ye doers of the word, and not hearers only, deceiving your own selves.

"For if any be a hearer of the word, and not a doer, he is like unto a man beholding his natural face in a glass:

"For he beholdeth himself, and goeth his way, and staightway forgetteth what manner of man he was."— Jas. 1:22–24.

As a sophomore in Bible college, I often listened to a popular fundamentalist pastor's daily radio program. One day he caught my attention with one of the most amazing statements I have ever heard (I remember it specifically because after I heard it, I wrote it down in the flyleaf of my Bible with his name beside it): "The longer I live, the more convinced I am that the key to a successful Christian life is living by schedule."

The concepts outlined in this book are life-changing. A decision to make Christlikeness the ultimate goal of your life is a wonderful decision, but it is only a starting place. To become a disciple of Christ requires discipline—the discipline to do, not just hear. Without a specific schedule and the character to follow that schedule, you will soon forget what you have learned by reading this book.

You must begin now. To help you, I have outlined a list of things to do to get you started. In no way do I believe that this is all that you must do to succeed, but it is a starting point. May God help you as you embark on the ultimate challenge. May Christ be formed in you!

Seven Things To Do Each Morning

(These should take about forty minutes.)

Every twelve-year-old should be given a loud alarm clock for his birthday. It is time to discover the great advantage of the quiet morning hours. I can get more work done in a few hours in the solitude of the early morn than in twice that amount of time midst the bustle and interruptions of midday. Start the race right! Get out of the blocks strong, and you will have a better chance of winning. Here are seven things to do each morning:

1. Ask God to help you be like Jesus. Pray specifically for these seven things:

Please give me the wisdom of Christ. I acknowledge that I lack wisdom, so I ask You to teach me Your wisdom today as I read and study and meditate on Your Word.

Please give me the mind of Christ. Help me to think the thoughts that You would think. Give me victory over daydreaming, foolish thoughts and wicked thinking.

Please give me the humility of Christ. Give me a servant's heart. Keep me humble before You today.

Please give me the speech of Christ. May all the words of my mouth be acceptable in Thy sight, O Lord, my strength and my redeemer.

Please give me the attitude of Christ. Make me teachable. Help me to react properly to instruction and rebuke. May I be a blessing to those who cross my path.

Please give me the courage of Christ—courage to do what is right even if I must do it alone, courage to share the Gospel with those who need to be saved.

Please give me the purity of Christ. Forgive me my sins. Keep me spiritually pure. Keep me physically pure. Protect and prepare the one you have created for me, and me for him/her.

2. Read one chapter of the Book of Proverbs. Proverbs is divided into thirty-one chapters. Read the one which corresponds with that day's date. If a month has fewer than thirty-one days, read to the end of the book on the last day of the month.

3. Write down one verse from this chapter in Proverbs on a 3x5 card. Carry this card with you throughout the day. Start by choosing a verse on wisdom or foolishness so you can become familiar with God's definition of both. Remember, this is also your weapon against the attacks of Satan.

4. Read one chapter of the Gospels. Begin with Matthew and read one chapter a day until you finish the Gospel of John, and then begin again. Think while you read. Picture everything that is happening. Become the thirteenth disciple. Question everything Jesus says or does. Learn how He thinks.

5. Write down one verse from this chapter from the Gospels on a 3x5 card. Throughout the day you can meditate on the person and works of Jesus Christ. No wicked thought can remain long in the presence of the King of Kings.

6. Review "The Ten Laws of Excellent Speech." Read each law and its corresponding Bible verses. Yield your tongue to the control of the Holy Spirit.

- Speak sparingly—Prov. 17:27; 10:19.
- Speak only after thinking—Prov. 29:20; Jas. 1:19.
- Speak honestly—Eph. 4:25; Prov. 12:17.
- Speak with grace—Col. 4:6.
- Speak only acceptable words—Ps. 19:14.
- Speak appropriately—Prov. 25:11; Eccles. 3:1.
- Speak respectfully—I Tim. 5:1, 2.

- Never speak evil of another person—Jas. 4:11; Titus 3:2.
- Never praise yourself—Prov. 27:2.
- Speak the Gospel boldly—Rom. 1:16.

7. Write one quick thank-you note or note of encouragement. Make a list of those who regularly invest in you. Thank them for their time and sacrifice. You don't have to write a long letter, just three to five sincere sentences.

Seven Things To do Each Evening

(This will take about one hour.)

"And the evening and the morning were the first day."—Gen. 1:5.

God's days are measured differently than ours. Unlike us, He starts each day in the evening. If you will read the first chapter of Genesis, I think you will agree that He was quite successful in His accomplishments using this formula. Much of the success of tomorrow is already determined by the time we go to bed tonight. Here are seven things to do each evening that will help you to develop the characteristics of the teenage Christ:

1. Study the Bible for thirty minutes each evening. Review the ten points in "A Guide to Studying the Bible" found in Chapter 3. Start with any topic in Proverbs, or you may want to choose one of the following: any part of the life of Christ (miracles, parables, etc.); the life of Samuel (favor of God and man); the life of David; the life of Mary; or word studies on *blessed/cursed*. The important thing is, choose one and get started!

2. Write down in a notebook all Bible principles

gleaned during these thirty minutes. You will be shocked how many times you will use these notes!

3. **Review and evaluate your success and failure at living like Christ that day.** Use your seven prayer requests from that morning. Did I display the wisdom of God? Did I have His mind? His humility? His speech? His attitude? His courage? His purity? God reviewed and evaluated His accomplishments at the end of each day of creation: "And God saw that it was good."

4. **Confess your shortcomings as sin and ask God to help you do better tomorrow.** This keeps you righteous before Him and in His favor.

5. **Evaluate each failure and determine how you can turn it into a success next time.** All of us fail, but we learn from our failures. If you did not handle a situation very well, decide specifically what you should have said or done differently.

6. **Make a "To do" list for the next day.** Set goals. Plan tomorrow tonight. As a young business tycoon, Charles Schwab asked Ivy Lee, a management consultant, to help him accomplish more each day and promised to pay him for a successful formula. Lee handed him a piece of paper and asked him to make a list of the things he needed to do the next day. Then he instructed him to number the items in order of their importance. Mr. Schwab did both.

"First thing tomorrow," he said to Mr. Schwab, "start working on number one and don't leave it until it is completed. Then take number two and stick with it until it is finished, and so on. Try this for a week, and if it works, send me what you think it is worth."

A few weeks later Mr. Schwab sent Mr. Lee a check for $25,000!

7. Give both parents a hug and kiss before you go to bed. Keep this relationship sweet. Never go to bed with something wrong between you and your parents.

Seven Things to Schedule Weekly

Every week each of us needs to have a time to reflect upon that which we have accomplished in the previous week. We need this time to evaluate our lives and rededicate ourselves to the commitments we have made to God. I believe that is one of the purposes God had in mind when He set aside a day of rest.

Here are some things you should do every week:

1. Attend all the services of your church. God has chosen to use the vehicle of preaching to display His power and wisdom (I Cor. 1:18–21). No one can claim to be like Jesus who does not faithfully attend church.

> *"And he [Jesus] came to Nazareth, where he had been brought up: and, as his custom was, he went into the synagogue on the sabbath day."*—Luke 4:16.

2. Be involved in a weekly soul-winning ministry of your church. Wisdom is the principal thing! God gives special wisdom to those who faithfully obey the Great Commission found in Matthew 28:19 and 20.

> *"The fruit of the righteous is a tree of life; and he that winneth souls is wise."*—Prov. 11:30.

3. Seek the counsel of the wise. Ask questions. Walk with great men. Like Christ, purposely seek out those who have spent a lifetime studying the Scriptures and living godly, separated lives. Each week, pick out a godly elderly person and ask him/her a question. Here are some suggestions:

• What is the secret to your long and happy marriage?

94

- What is your favorite Bible verse and why?

- Is there a quote that you have written down somewhere that has helped you in your life?

- What was the greatest thing your mother ever taught you? your father? your grandparents?

- Who led you to the Lord?

- What is the most important character trait I should work on as a teenager?

It is sad and amazing how many teenagers walk right by men and women every Sunday who have great resources of wisdom and never even stop to shake their hands.

4. Review the ten traits of a slothful teenager. Once a week evaluate yourself in this area and work hard at eliminating any tendencies toward laziness. Review the Scriptures found in Chapter 7 that correspond to these questions:

- Do you often fail to take care of the things that have been provided for you?

- Are you constantly asking your parents to buy you things?

- Do you make excuses to get out of doing your work?

- Is your bedroom generally untidy and unorganized?

- Do you sleep more than is absolutely necessary?

- Do you have to be reminded to do your simple daily chores?

- Do you have a lot of idle time?

- Do you work harder when a teacher is watching you?

- Do you look for reasons to put off doing a job?

- Are you too conceited to be absolutely honest in

answering the above questions?

5. Review the six character traits adults respect in teenagers. Then ask yourself, "Am I more concerned with what adults think of me, or my peers? Am I being an example of the believer in my speech, in my behavior, in my love, in my attitude, in my faith and in my purity?"

- Adults respect excellent speech.
- Adults respect mature behavior.
- Adults respect selfless love.
- Adults respect a good attitude.
- Adults respect sincere faith.
- Adults respect wholesome purity.

6. Review the character traits of the foolish man. As you read these, carefully examine your own life. Declare war on any foolish tendencies that have crept into your personality. Then read the list again and examine closely the lives of the people with whom you spend the most time. Remember, God promises that a companion of fools shall be destroyed.

A foolish man can be identified by how he acts (all references are from Proverbs):

—despises reproof: 17:10
—despises instruction: 15:5
—sees mischief as sport: 10:23
—makes a mock of sin: 14:9
—meddles in others' affairs: 20:3
—despises his parents: 15:20; 19:13
—perceives himself as always right: 12:15; 14:16
—quick-tempered: 12:16; 14:16, 17; 27:3

A foolish man can be identified by how he talks:

—slanders others: 10:18
—double-tongued: 10:18
—perverse lips: 19:1
—speaks before he thinks: 29:11
—rod of pride: 14:3
—proclaims foolishness: 12:23; 15:2,14
—contentious: 18:6

7. Schedule a learning opportunity with a skilled craftsman in your church. These opportunities should be scheduled by your parents or with their permission. Remember, the younger you are, the more limited these opportunities will be; but as you prove yourself and gain a reputation as a hard worker, you will soon find that you will be sought out when someone needs a hand.

The most important key to living the Christian life successfully may well be living by a schedule. What is not kept before us is soon forgotten. Desiring to live like Jesus cannot be just a fad or a phase. It must be the most important goal of life, a goal that will only be reached when we discipline ourselves to live on purpose and on schedule.

9
Glorious Even in Failure

To be like Jesus—this is the ultimate goal.

Years ago I read a simple quote that I have never forgotten: "Some goals are so worthy that it is glorious even to fail."

For years I have pursued the elusive and glorious goal of being like Christ. I have failed a thousand times in a thousand different ways. At times I have been tempted to lower the bar, to adjust my dream to something more easily attainable. When I have yielded to this temptation, my fleshly ego has been appeased, but my spirit eventually begins to cry out in utter disgust. What satisfaction is there in obtaining a counterfeit! So, again I would raise the standard, and again I would begin to fail. But in the process, at times I would find myself at heights that I would never have experienced if I had tried to reach for anything less. To strive for perfection and fail is infinitely more glorious than to spend my life living a lie and pretending to be content.

Every day when I awake, I face the ultimate challenge. I live, while many around me seem content to exist. I have learned much about my own weakness and much more about God's strength. And occasionally, there have been those times—during the delivery of a sermon when self seems to have vanished and I have joined the crowd in listening to the message from

God; or at a prayer meeting when we have tarried long enough to begin to bear the anguish of His burden and feel as it were the cool breezes of Gethsemane's garden; or while stopping strangers on hot, summer streets to offer them Living Water; when I have heard a voice so distinct that it is clearer than sound, directing me to a particular house or person; or in my office, in solitude, but not alone, studying the Bible with such frenzied fervor that I have forgotten the clock on the wall and everything else bound by its mortal ticks, hearing nothing but my Tutor instructing me and amazing me with the depth of His wisdom—glorious, wonderful moments, when I have been allowed to touch the hem of His garment! Moments when a still, small voice whispers into my spirit's ear, "This is it. This is what it is like to be like Him!"

It is glorious! Glorious to succeed and, yes, glorious even to fail! This is the essence of a true believer's existence. This is the breath of Heaven and the taste of immortality.

This is the ultimate.

Settle for nothing less.

IO

A Brief Word to Parents

As parents, every one of us will choose some pattern to follow in the rearing of our children. Many parents look to the world's definition of success and use it as the pattern for their children's upbringing. Others try to mimic what they see other parents doing. Still others are busy trying to rear their children in their own image. After all, "I did this and that when I was young, and it didn't hurt me!"

I contend that there is a better pattern than any of these—and that pattern is the Lord Jesus Christ.

"My little children, of whom I travail in birth again until Christ be formed in you."—Gal. 4:19.

Our job as parents is to do everything possible to see to it that our children's hearts and minds are molded to the image of Christ. This is the ultimate goal and the ultimate challenge. To choose any other pattern, even that of ourselves, is to rob our children of some of what they could one day become.

The priorities of Christ's teenage years have been outlined in this book. They are placed in the Bible for a reason. If you are honest, as you look around you, you would agree that these are not the same priorities that occupy the heart and time of the average Christian teenager. As parents, we must bear the responsibility for this.

Wisdom, maturity, favor of God, favor of men, submission and work—how can we help our children develop these priorities in their lives?

Wisdom

Wisdom: the ability and willingness to base all of our thinking, our actions and our decisions on the principles of God's Word.

Decide that God is right when He said that "wisdom is the principal thing." Biblical wisdom is more important than academic knowledge. A student can make straight As and still not be wise. The world is full of educated fools. I am very much for a child's getting a good education; however, it mystifies me as to why some parents spend endless time and money ensuring that their children get a good education yet allow them to remain ignorant when it comes to God's Word.

Take your children to church. Teach them the Bible at home. If possible, get them in a Christian school that places as much emphasis on biblical wisdom as it does on academic excellence.

Maturity

If I were to ask you to list the stages of development in a person's life, most would write down the following: child, teenager, young adult, middle age, senior citizen.

Now, let's compare this list to the stages of development listed in the Scriptures.

> "I write unto you, fathers, because ye have known him that is from the beginning. I write unto you, young men, because ye have overcome the wicked one. I write unto you, little children, because ye have known the Father."—I John 2:13.

"That the aged men be sober, grave, temperate, sound in faith, in charity, in patience.

"The aged women likewise, that they be in behaviour as becometh holiness, not false accusers, not given to much wine, teachers of good things;

"That they may teach the young women to be sober, to love their husbands, to love their children,

"To be discreet, chaste, keepers at home, good, obedient to their own husbands, that the word of God be not blasphemed.

"Young men likewise exhort to be sober minded."—Titus 2:2–6.

God's list of maturity development—children, young men and women, aged men and women—looks different than ours.

We have invented two additional stages dedicated to immaturity and irresponsibility: the teenager and the adult in mid-life crisis! Then we combine the two. Most adults reach their mid-life crisis during the same time that their kids have become teenagers. Now everyone in the family has an excuse to go crazy!

During these years, many families forget the Bible principles they have always believed, throw away the principles of separation from the world and 'do that which is right in their own eyes' (Judg. 17:6). The pastor, who has helped them through so many crises when the kids were younger, suddenly doesn't know anything! And woe to anyone who points out to this family that they are getting off track. After all, they all have an excuse.

No, we do not have an excuse! God labels our proper development differently. He has designed a boy to be first a child, then a young man and then an aged man. He has set the pattern for a girl to become first a child, then a young woman and then an aged woman. Immaturity after childhood is our invention, not God's intention.

I can remember my grandparents' talking about growing up during the Depression. "We didn't have a childhood," they would say. Many of them didn't. Because of their financial circumstances, they worked hard and grew up fast. Some of them vowed that their children would have the childhood they did not have.

Over the past two generations, the pendulum has swung too far the other way. For many, childhood has been extended all the way into their college years. There has to be a balance. And I believe that the example of Christ provides us with this balance.

Your child's twelfth birthday is an important milestone in his life. This is the age that Jesus stepped from childhood into manhood. This is when He began to increase in maturity. This is our example. Both parents should be involved in planning and participating in a special day for their child when he turns twelve. Take him to a nice restaurant. There are several things that you should discuss with him on this important day:

1. If you have not discussed sex with your child, this is the age to do it. I know that this is awkward for many parents, but it is important that this information come from you. Many Christians oppose the sex education that is going on in our public schools (and well they should!) but then fail to educate their children themselves.

There are helpful resources that you can acquire to give to your child to read a few days before you talk to him, but be sure you follow up by talking to him yourself. Talk to him about the importance of abstinence and purity. Explain to him your timetable and rules of courtship and how these will help him achieve his goal of one day having a happy marriage.

2. Talk to him about the example of Jesus Christ. Give him a copy of this book to read a few weeks before this important day. Discuss the six priorities of the teenage years of our Saviour. Help him set up a schedule so that he has time set aside to develop in all of these areas.

Remember that at age twelve, Jesus began to increase in these areas. He did not come to maturity overnight, and it would be wrong to expect that from our children.

3. Explain that in some ways your relationship to him will begin to change. I believe it is important that we begin to treat our children differently at this age. They need to be treated more like young men and women and less like children; and in return, they should be expected to increase in mature behavior.

4. List for him specifically the increase of privileges that will accompany his acceptance of increased responsibility. Increased rewards should accompany an increase in maturity. Outline one major reward for each of his next five birthdays, each one increasing his privileges.

5. Give him a special gift, a keepsake, that will forever remind him of this special day. What a tremendous time in a child's life! This will not only be a milestone in his life but also a milestone in your relationship with him. This is the age when we begin to help him develop mature speech, mature understanding and mature thinking.

Finding Favor With God and Man

"Let not mercy and truth forsake thee: bind them about thy neck; write them upon the table of thine heart:

"So shalt thou find favour and good understanding in the sight of God and man."—Prov. 3:3, 4.

Perhaps the hardest thing for most teenagers to achieve is balance. Come to think of it, that may be the hardest thing for any of us to achieve. We need both mercy and truth. Both are to be worn around our necks and written upon our hearts. As parents, we need mercy and truth to rear children who will be like Christ.

Sometimes we have the truth but forget the mercy. Remember that the ultimate goal is also an impossible one. Your children are going to fall short. So do we. It is kind of amazing when a professional baseball player with a batting average of .400 (four hits for every ten times at bat) will receive trophies and accolades, even if he struck out the other six times.

A young person who is trying to live for the Lord is not always going to succeed. I know good kids whose success-to-failure ratio is much better than forty percent, but they hardly ever hear any applause when they succeed—only correction when they fail. If they fail in the act of trying, extra training and encouragement will go a lot further than punishment. We need truth, but we also need mercy.

The other extreme is when we put on the ornament of mercy and forget the truth. As parents, we cannot lay aside the truths of God's Word in the name of mercy. Compassion works within the boundaries of the laws of God, never outside them. Be careful that you do not find yourself always making excuses for your children and failing to recognize and correct foolish tendencies.

Submission

Obedience is paramount in a child's development. The foolish man knows what God wants him to do but refuses to do it. Foolishness is bound in the heart of a child, and you can see it early. It will not take him long to try to see what will happen when he directly disobeys you. A parent who ignores the teachings in Proverbs on child rearing will one day have his heart broken by his child.

However, obedience and submission can be two different things. Obedience is an outward compliance to your commands. Submission is an inward respect for your position and authority.

"My son, forget not my law; but let thine heart keep my commandments."—Prov. 3:1.

A teenager can obey with his hands and rebel in his heart. Submission comes with understanding.

"A man of understanding is of an excellent spirit."— Prov. 17:27.

When your child turns twelve, more time needs to be spent explaining the "why's" of the Christian life. Sometimes we contribute to the problem of rebellion by refusing to take the time to show our kids the Bible basis behind the rules and convictions by which we live. When they begin to develop an understanding heart, their attitudes will improve.

Submission is as much *caught* as *taught.* Our children watch what we do more than they listen to what we say. Submission is first taught by example. If we constantly rebel against the authorities that God has placed over us, our instruction to them will carry little weight.

Never criticize or undermine other authority figures

in your child's life. Back up his teachers, principal, youth pastor and especially his pastor. You cannot teach selective rebellion. Authority is a constant. If your children are allowed to criticize these people when they are not around, your children will also criticize you when you're not around.

Work

Wise is the parent who teaches his children to work. To a young child, work is just another game. It is an opportunity to spend time with you. Daddy goes out to work on a project—

"What are you going to do, Dad?"

"I've got to fix the mower."

"Can I help?"

Little girls stand up on a chair beside their mothers, helping them wash the dishes. They want to help Mom with everything she does.

At some point, they begin to see work as a drudgery. Why does their attitude change? Maybe they have listened to us complain about work so much that they decide it must be unpleasant. I don't know. I do believe that our children will adopt our attitudes toward work.

Teach your children that work is noble. Let them experience the satisfaction of finishing a job—and doing it right. Convince them that the taste of sweat is sweet and sore muscles are a sign of honor. Never allow them to shirk their assigned responsibility or do less than their best. A job worth doing is worth doing right—the first time.

Teach them the skills necessary to make a living. Involve them in simple home repairs, and you will have saved them thousands of dollars over their lifetime. Teach them to use and respect tools. Don't belittle their lack of knowledge—no one knows until he is taught. Encourage them, and one day they will bless your name.

Finally, teach them common sense. This is accomplished by teaching them how to think through a problem. Don't be so quick to answer their questions. Instead, ask questions that will guide them toward the answer but will still require them to think. Help them to a solution, but don't just give it to them. They need to struggle some in order to grow.

My wife recently helped our youngest daughter with a school science fair project. Her chosen subject was this: "How do baby chickens hatch?" For four weeks our utility room was converted into a chicken hatchery!

The person who gave us the chicken eggs also gave us a wealth of information on successfully hatching them. One caution he gave us was, "When the chickens begin to hatch out of the eggs, no matter how long it takes them or how sorry you feel for them, do not help them out of the shells." He explained that the strength they develop while fighting their way out is what will keep them alive when they finally make it.

It is extremely hard as a parent not to run to your child's rescue every time he faces a challenge or difficulty. I know some who would say that to do so proves you are a good parent.

We should be there for them, but I believe that many times we interfere with what God is trying to teach them. By "cracking the egg" for them, we may be robbing them of the strength and maturity that they would gain by working it out for themselves. Give advice and encouragement, but remember, they need to overcome some things on their own.

It will take courage to decide that Jesus will be the pattern for your child's teenage years. You will be shocked at the criticism you will receive, not just from the world but from Christians who have adopted the world's priorities as the pattern for their children. It has never been easy to live by the Word of God.

The reward is watching Christ formed in them, watching them later in life making decisions based on biblical principles instead of mindlessly following the crowd.

May God give each of you the wisdom and courage to raise your children to the glory of God.

II
A Brief Word to Youth Workers

I thank God for the great army of Christians who have dedicated themselves to working with teenagers: pastors, youth pastors, church laymen, Sunday school teachers, Christian school teachers, principals, music directors, coaches and many others who take time to invest in the lives of young people. It is a noble and important work that you do.

I love to spend time with anyone who has a true burden for teenagers. As iron sharpeneth iron, I have learned so much by spending time with other youth workers. I love to ask them questions—questions about their youth programs, youth activities, youth banquet ideas, youth revivals and conferences. I become enraptured when hearing success stories of young people who have overcome great obstacles to live for the Lord. I can also share the tears over a young person who has gone astray. For over twenty years my wife and I have been investing in teenagers. We know the joy, and we know the heartache.

Above all, I love to talk to youth workers about their philosophy of youth work. By philosophy, I mean the principles behind the program—their master plan or master pattern.

There should be a "why" behind every detail of a youth program. What greater master plan to follow than the plan of our Master? Whose pattern are you now following? In whose likeness are your teenagers being formed?

Wisdom

Every saved person who works with young people has a scriptural mandate to teach them wisdom. It should be the *principal thing* of your youth program. There is no greater favor you can do for a teenager.

Wisdom comes from the Word of God. Biblical instruction needs to be the cornerstone of our youth programs. Jesus and the Word of God are synonymous! He *is* the Word. Christlikeness is learned through studying the Scriptures.

I'm afraid that many youth programs have devolved into glorified baby-sitting services. We spend most of our time entertaining teens instead of instructing them. Teenagers can learn to love the Scriptures. If we make the Word of God exciting and meaningful to them, they can learn wisdom.

Maturity

Provide your youth group with an example of maturity. There is one at every youth conference or teen camp. Here he comes—Brother Teenybopper, youth pastor extraordinaire! He dresses like his teens, talks like his teens, wears his hair like his teens (and sometimes even an earring!), sneers at the rules of the program like his teens. He is not here to debate; he is here to relate. His speech mimics theirs. He adjusts his understanding and thinking to their level. His philosophy is simple: you reach teenagers by becoming one of them.

What he does not realize is that he is not reaching them; they have reached him. They may like him, but they don't respect him.

Our scriptural responsibility is to help bring young people to maturity. The Bible is very clear on what this entails. Teens need to be encouraged to put away childish speech, childish understanding and childish thinking. This is never accomplished by immature leadership.

I am all for having fun with our teenagers and for planning activities that they will enjoy. However, I detest the notion that you reach them by becoming one of them. Young men need a godly man to look up to, not a worldly, undisciplined imitation of themselves. Young ladies need a virtuous woman to follow, not a painted, immodest "teenage wanna-be."

I'm afraid this same misguided philosophy is behind the movement in many of our churches to provide alternative, contemporary services to reach young people. Some think that if we adjust to their dress, their music and their thinking, we can convince them to become Christians.

In doing so, we ignore the biblical principle of separation from the world. The church that becomes worldly in an effort to reach the world is not conquering; instead, it has been conquered. The greatest attraction to Christianity is in its uniqueness from the world. It is our clear and obvious difference from them that grabs their attention and gives us the right to promote a better way.

> "Looking for that blessed hope, and the glorious appearing of the great God and our Saviour Jesus Christ;
>
> "Who gave himself for us, that he might redeem us from all iniquity, and purify unto himself a peculiar people, zealous of good works."—Titus 2:13, 14.

Favor With God And Men

Most young people begin to backslide when they want to win the favor of the wrong people. They want to be accepted by a carnal or unsaved crowd, so they begin to talk and act in whatever way is necessary to win their favor. Often winning a boyfriend's or girlfriend's approval becomes more important than staying in favor with God and their parents.

The heart's desire of every young person ought to be to please the Lord and win the favor of godly adults. This is the example provided for us by the teenage Christ. If a teenager will adopt Christlikeness as his ultimate goal, he then will strive to do those things that will please Him.

As youth workers, we need constantly to point teenagers to Christ. In our preaching and teaching, we need to emphasize the importance of pleasing the Lord. Often we need to take them to Calvary, to remind them of the great sacrifice that He made to redeem them.

"Well, it's my life, and I'll live it the way I want!" No, it's not your life. You have been bought with a price. In gratitude to our Lord for the great salvation He has provided you, you are to honor and please Him above all.

Submission to Parents

As youth pastors, it is our job to do everything possible to strengthen the bond between the teenager and his parents. To do anything else is unscriptural and self-serving. Shame on you if the teenagers of your church are closer to you than they are to their mothers and fathers. We need to help the parents, not try to take their place.

A Brief Word to Youth Workers

1. Never criticize a teenager's parents. This tears down their authority in that child's eyes. Publicly and privately point out their strengths to their children. Help make their parents their heroes.

2. Point your teenagers to their parents when they seek your counsel. When teenagers come to me for counsel, I always ask, "Have you sought the counsel of your parents on this matter?" If they have not, I ask them to go home and get their advice. If they still need to talk to me, my door is open.

If they have already talked to their parents, I always ask, "What did they say you should do?" I am not going to give advice opposite what their parents have given. If I disagree with their advice, I will never tell the teenager. If I feel it is important enough, I will talk to their parents and work through them.

Parents are the final authority in the life of that child, and we are wrong if we do not respect that.

3. Plan an annual Parent Appreciation Night. This is one of the highlights of the year for our youth group. The parents receive invitations in the mail to this special event. We have our young people fix them their favorite desserts and serve as their waiters and waitresses. After they have eaten, the teenagers put on a program that includes a mixture of humorous skits and serious testimonies. Throughout the evening, each teenager has an opportunity to honor his parents with a song, a poem or in some other creative way.

Parents love this, and they will carry these memories with them forever.

4. Plan some activities that include the parents.

5. On other activities, use some of the parents as chaperones.

6. Do not plan too many activities. People need family time. Encourage the parents to do things with their children. The best childhood memories should be of time spent with their parents, not with their youth pastor.

7. Be submissive to the senior pastor of your church. Teenagers have hypocrisy radar. They will watch to see if you practice what you preach. A youth pastor who thinks he knows more than the pastor and refuses to submit to his authority is no different than a rebellious teenager who thinks he knows more than his parents.

Mastering a Wage-Earning Skill

Warning! I'm about to tear down the golden calf of most Christian schools and youth programs. *Basketball is a game. Softball is a game. Football is a game. Volleyball is a game.* **Working for a living is real life.**

If we are going to dress up our girls as cheerleaders and have them cheer our young men, then let them cheer the ones who work after-school jobs. Load these young ladies in a van, take them to the yard where a young man is mowing and let them cheer his efforts to earn the money to attend a Christian school.

The heroes of our youth groups should not be the young men who can score the most points on a basketball court but the young men who are most like Christ.

Jesus worked alongside Joseph and spent His youth mastering a wage-earning skill. His body gained the strength and endurance that can only be achieved through hard, physical labor. (There is a *huge* difference between playing hard for an hour and working hard for ten hours.) Jesus learned common sense, reasoning, and the ability to think through a project from start to finish. His eye became sharp, His hands skilled, and His back strong to the task.

At eighteen years of age, He was not known as the best point guard in Nazareth but as the best young carpenter in town. When Joseph died, Mary didn't have to go to work. There was still a Man in the family, a Man capable, ready and able to provide for His mother and younger siblings.

May God help us to rear a generation of young men and young ladies who have the desire to work and the skills to make a living.

I have, on purpose, challenged you to think about the philosophy behind your youth program. Write out your objectives and the scriptural basis for these goals. If you were the first person who ever started a youth program in a church and you did not have other programs to copy—you had only the Word of God to guide you—would the emphasis of your program be different?

We tell our young people to stop following the crowd—instead, to base their beliefs and actions on the Word of God. Well?

12
"About My Father's Business"

"And he said unto them, How is it that ye sought me? wist ye not that I must be about my Father's business?"— Luke 2:49.

At twelve years of age, Jesus had to remind His mother gently that there was a purpose, a *cause*, for which He had been sent to earth. At this tender age, He had become convinced that nothing was more important than finding and accomplishing the "business" that His Father had sent Him to do.

From the age of twelve until the age of thirty, He set out to do those things that would prepare Him to accomplish the will of His Father.

This book has been written to remind us that God has some "business" that He has created for each of us to accomplish for Him. The priorities we set, the goals we pursue in our teenage years are important! God has not left us clueless as to what these goals should be.

May God raise up a generation of teenagers who are full of wisdom; teenagers who are mature in their words, thoughts and understanding; young women who have the ability to please God and gain the respect of godly adults; young men who realize early in life that manhood is never reached through rebellion; young people who are not afraid to work and are humble enough to be taught how to labor skillfully.

May God raise up young Christlike teenagers. And may the world see it and marvel!

For a complete list of
available books,
please go to

swordofthelord.com.